MW01199166

THE SCENICLAND RADIO

A Travel Adventure
in Search of the
New Zealand Experience

In loving memory of F.E.

Copyright

The Scenicland Radio:
A Travel Adventure in Search of the New Zealand Experience

ISBN: 9780645118728
Imprint: Simon Michael Prior
10 9 8 7 6 5 4 3 2 1

Contents

1. CONUNDRUM

The dog finds it first.

He sniffs a dark-red stain on the garden path.
I hesitate.

Knife.
Upside-down tin hat.
Ladder splayed across the lawn.
What happened here?

The farmhouse door bangs in the wind.
Kitchen.
Chopping board.
Half-sliced onion.
Knocked-over dining chair.
Where is everyone?
Am I alone?
And what am I going to do about the cows?

2. A HUMAN SACRIFICE

"Ladies and Gentlemen, we will shortly be arriving at Auckland International Airport. In preparation for landing, please ensure your seat back is upright, your tray table is stowed, and your armrest is down."

"Far out, Simon. What are you doing? Stop leaning over me."

"I want to see the sheep."

"What sheep?"

"All the sheep which live in New Zealand. But I can't see any yet. We're still flying over the sea."

Fiona stuffed her magazine in the seat pocket. "At least you stopped babbling about the Queen of Tonga when you dropped off to sleep about an hour ago."

She pulled a band from around her wrist and tied her dark-red hair in a ponytail. "I can't believe I'll be back in New Zealand today after over two years. I wonder if Mum and Dad'll have changed."

I clasped my hands together and stared into my lap.

Eighteen months ago, in 1995, I'd met Fiona in London. Immigration issues had almost split us apart, forced us to flee my homeland, and escape to her country.

I loved her.

I wanted to be with her forever.

But would her family accept a boy from a big English city? A boy accustomed to parking meters, office blocks, rainy pavements, and traffic lights.

Fiona stemmed from rural stock.

Farming people from the South Island's West Coast.

The most remote, rural region of the country.

Will they like me? How will I fit in? I don't know anything about farming.

Fiona held my arm. "What's on your mind?"

The plane window offered a view of the morning sun's golden arms, stretched across the horizon like a margarine advertisement. Butterflies twitched in my stomach as I chose my words. I didn't want her to know my concerns.

"It's incredible to think I'm going to live in New Zealand for the next year," I said. "I've never been away from England for more than a few weeks. New Zealand's close to Australia, right, so it'll feel hot?"

Fiona laughed. "It's not as hot as Australia. It'll be sunnier than London, though."

"I thought you said it's wet where your family lives?"

"The West Coast's renowned for its weather," she said. "But it's not as wet as the JAFAs maintain."

"JAFAs?"

"Just Another, err, Flipping Aucklander. It's what West Coast New Zealanders call city people."

City people.

JAFAs.

The farmers even have a derogatory nickname for us.

The gap between the sun and the horizon widened. A long band of white cloud stretched across the sea, smearing the light-blue sky like a toddler's finger painting.

The Air New Zealand jet circled.

"Cabin crew, take your seats for landing."

I heard the wheels extract.

Fiona grinned and jiggled in her seat, as fields and houses appeared below.

With a sudden thump, the aircraft touched the runway.

She smiled and grasped my hand.

"This is it. Your new home."

I still hadn't seen any sheep.

≈≈≈

"It's always miles between the plane and immigration," said Fiona. "Why can't they put them next to each other?"

Two red stripes burnt where the cabin baggage straps scored my hand. I clenched and unclenched my palm, swapped hands, and picked it up again.

Beads of sweat formed on my forehead as we advanced towards the uniformed agents perched in the immigration kiosks. At this point in any journey, I worried that, like a tense scene in a 1970s John le Carré drama, border security officers dressed as the Gestapo would escort me to a side room and take turns to interrogate me.

I kicked the hand luggage along the floor, as we queued for Checkpoint Charlie.

"Good morning, may I see your passports, please?"

The immigration lady opened Fiona's dark-blue New Zealand passport and flicked through the pages. The silver fern on its cover flashed in the stark lighting.

"Hi, Fiona," she said, as if they were old friends. "Welcome home."

"Thank you, and I've brought an Englishman back with me."

"Hello, Englishman," said the lady.

I smiled cautiously.

The lady opened my British passport. She scrutinised my photo, inspected me, and flicked to the page with my working holiday visa sticker.

"Welcome to New Zealand, Simon. I'm sure you'll love it here. Your visa lasts one year. If you'd like to stay longer, be sure to leave plenty of time to apply for a new one before it runs out."

"Erm, okay. I will."

The immigration lady picked up her rubber stamp. "Where are you travelling to?"

Don't give anything away, Fiona. It might be a trap.

"The West Coast of the South Island," said Fiona. "It's my home."

"Oh, wow," said the agent. Her stamp thumped on Fiona's passport. "D'you know Eileen McKinnon?"

"I think so. Is she married to Ron?"

"That's right," said the immigration lady. "She's my aunt."

She stamped my passport and returned them both. "Nice to meet you both," she said. "Enjoy your journey home." She looked behind us. "Next, please."

We crossed no man's land between the agents' cubicles. I clutched my chest and exhaled.

"I can't believe how friendly she was. She encouraged me to stay longer."

"New Zealand's more relaxed than England. I bet within a few months you'll forget you're a city boy, and you'll lose your English reserve."

≈≈≈

"What could I buy your parents for having me to stay?"

"We purchased those tropical fish napkin rings in Tonga. Mum might appreciate them."

"What about your dad?"

"Whisky."

"Is he a regular whisky drinker?"

"He's known for it."

Maybe Fiona's dad will like me if I drink whisky with him. I don't know what it tastes like.

"We could buy whisky here," said Fiona. She tugged my hand, and I blinked under the bright lights of duty-free.

I groaned. I hoped Fiona's need to fondle every item on sale wouldn't mean we missed our domestic flight on to Christchurch.

Multiple scents assaulted my nostrils, as we navigated displays of exotic and erotic shaped glass bottles balanced on piles of bright packaging.

A middle-aged blonde lady in a white laboratory coat approached. "Would you like to try Elizabeth Arden's 5th avenue?" she asked.

She brandished a small bottle at chest height and smiled with perfect white teeth embedded in Coke logo-coloured lipstick.

"Ooh, yes, please," said Fiona. She smiled, pulled her sleeve up, and offered her wrist to the perfume vendor. I knew from experience she'd sample every fragrance, whether or not she chose to purchase any, so I excused myself from the proceedings and headed for a wall of bottle-filled glass shelves.

I plopped the hand luggage at my feet.

Grant's. Jameson. Famous Grouse. Bell's.

Which brand would impress Fiona's dad?

I glanced over my shoulder to find an assistant.

Johnny Walker Black Label.

Johnny Walker Red Label.

The only difference I could perceive was the price.

I pulled bank notes from my pocket and read the numbers on the unfamiliar, multi-coloured currency. It reminded me of collecting £200 as I passed 'Go'.

A luminous, star-shaped sticker on a lower shelf promoted a light-brown, stumpy bottle with a tan-coloured top.

Fiona touched my shoulder. She smelt like the ground floor of Selfridge's during a particularly pushy Estée Lauder promotion.

I showed her the bottle.

"This one's on special," I said. "If we buy two, we save twenty per cent."

"Dad won't thank you for giving him Chivas Regal; it's a blend. He only drinks single malt."

I scrutinised the bottles, frowned, and shrugged.

"There isn't one called single malt."

Fiona placed her finger flat on her lips and ran her eyes along the shelves. She plucked a tall, gold box from the top shelf and thrust it into my arms.

"Glenmorangie. It's a single malt."

She paid the cashier. I held the Glenmorangie to my chest like a breastfeeding baby.

"Can you wait here with the bags?" asked Fiona. "I'm popping to the ladies."

I placed the whisky on top of the hand luggage and idled outside a bookshop.

A front cover displayed a photograph of eight young people wearing green lifejackets and red helmets. Their mouths wide, they paddled a yellow, inflatable raft through alarming-looking, serrated rocks. I narrowed my eyebrows, picked up the guide, and skimmed the description.

New Zealand.

Ice-blue lakes.

Snow-covered mountains.

Verdant rainforests.

My fingers ran over the shiny back cover. A map showed the country's position in the world.

Isolated.

Remote.

Outlying.

Scary.

≈≈≈

"Have you just arrived in Auckland?" asked a sturdy lady with brown skin and dark hair. She smiled from behind the bookshop counter.

Her accent's stronger than Fiona's.

"Yep, I've flown in from London with my Kiwi girlfriend. I'm living here for a year."

"Choice!" She laughed, revealing gaps in her teeth, and stuffed the guide into a paper bag. "You'll be needing this. Welcome to *Aotearoa.*"

A-o-te-a-ro-a? I wonder what that means?

She handed me my change, and I opened the guide.

New Zealand, the book stated, considered itself the world's extreme outdoor sports centre. Travellers could choose from thrilling activities, such as swimming with wild dolphins, rafting down white-water rivers, hiking up remote glaciers, skydiving from small planes, and jettisoning off high bridges.

New Zealand's population of under four million, continued the guide, primarily lived in the North Island. The South Island was far more sparsely inhabited, and many locals referred to it as 'the village'. Remoter parts contained the last reserves of wild kiwi birds.

I remembered a promise I'd made to my father.

Fiona returned from the bathroom, and I showed her my purchase.

"Why d'you waste money on that?" she asked. "I come from here, and I've never needed a guidebook."

"I should do some research. I don't want people to think I'm a complete novice. For instance, what does *A-o-te-a-ro-a* mean? The shop lady said it to me."

"It's the Māori word for New Zealand. It means *Land of the Long White Cloud.*"

"Will I need to know many Māori words?" I glanced back at the shop. "Should I buy a phrase book as well?"

Fiona took my hand. "Stop fretting. This is my country. You're with me."

≈≈≈

"Welcome on board, sir. 27E and F? Straight down, on the left-hand side."

Richard Clayderman-type background music accompanied the donk-donk-donk of the hand luggage bumping down the aisle of the connecting flight to Christchurch. I smiled at a lady sitting in our row.

She pushed down on the armrests to help herself stand, then stepped into the aisle. Her permed, brown hair framed a face covered with several kilos of make-up, trowelled into deep, fleshy wrinkles.

Fiona manoeuvred into the window seat. I followed her, and the lady squished in beside me. My body tilted to allow her to overflow across the armrest.

"Do you two live in Christchurch?" she asked.

She wore a smart shirt with small red checks, and her collar turned up stiffly, as if it had suffered a nasty accident with a starch bottle.

Fiona leant forward and spoke across me. "I've lived overseas for the last two years. I met my partner in London, and he's going to stay with me on the West Coast."

The lady's eyebrows shot up and disappeared under her fringe.

"Really?" she asked, as if Fiona had offered me as a human sacrifice.

"It's a good job she's taking you there," the lady whispered conspiratorially to me. "The West Coast would benefit from some fresh blood."

I clenched my teeth and sucked in a breath. I hoped Fiona hadn't heard.

The lady paused and inclined her head towards me again.

"I hope you enjoy torrential rain, though. On the west side of the mountains, it can last for weeks."

I felt a jolt as the plane pushed back from the gate.

"Ladies and Gentlemen, even if you have flown with us many times, every plane is different. Please watch this brief safety demonstration before we take off."

I gave the hostess my full attention, as she dangled a bright-yellow oxygen mask and shoved her head through a luminous lifejacket. I noted the light and the whistle for attracting attention. At her instruction, I checked the location of my nearest exit and counted how many rows of passengers I would need to trample in the unlikely event of an emergency.

The plane taxied, turned round, and accelerated, and I dipped into my new guidebook at the section on the West Coast.

The West Coast, it began, also known as Westland, should more accurately be called 'wet-land' as over five metres of rain fell annually. The region consisted of a 600-kilometre untamed, rugged strip of land, sandwiched between tall mountains and the Tasman Sea, and inhabited by untamed, rugged people.

I considered Fiona's choice of duty-free for her father and wondered whether a man who insisted on single malt whisky was as untamed and rugged as the guide suggested.

The West Coast scenery, the guide continued, comprised soaring, snow-capped peaks and unclimbed foothills, impenetrable forests, lakes fringed with pine trees, and wild, desolate beaches dotted with twisting, architectural driftwood. The region was so picturesque, the local radio station had been named Scenicland FM.

I bit down on a smile, stared out of the plane's window, frowned and pointed.

"What are those broad, grey, twisty lines?"

Fiona lowered her magazine and followed my finger.

"They're rivers."

"They don't look like rivers; they're not blue."

"It's summer. You're seeing the pebble riverbed. When the rivers flood, the entire area will be a rushing, dirty torrent."

"And where are all the sheep?" I said. "I thought New Zealand had millions of sheep."

"Everyone farms cows where I come from. Cows and deer."

"Don't New Zealanders live on roast lamb?"

"Our family never buys it. Mum hates the smell."

I gazed at the backbone of jagged peaks, plopped on the landscape like a primary school papier-mâché project.

"Can we see the West Coast from here?"

"It's over those mountains. A long drive across the pass."

Mountain pass.

Mountains.

Giant, papier-mâché mountains.

Mountains that would separate the city boy from the cities.

My skin tingled as I experienced the first uncomfortable indication I'd be living a very long way from the nearest McDonald's.

$$\approx \approx \approx$$

"Ladies and Gentlemen, we will shortly be landing in Christchurch. Please return to your seats, ensure your seat back is upright, your tray table is up, and your armrest is down."

I shuffled in my seat and bit my nails.

"Will all your family meet us at the airport?"

"Dad won't. He'll be working on the farm, helping Phillip with the milking."

"Phillip's your eldest brother, right?"

"Yep. He undertakes most of the farm work now Dad's semi-retired. Mum'll collect us today. She doesn't enjoy farming any more. She helps when it's busy in calving time."

Calving time. I wonder when that is.

"And Mum might bring my sister with her."

"Does she work on the farm, too?"

Fiona laughed. "No, Angela's still at school. She's seventeen. Colin, my middle brother, might come to the airport to say hello. He's the mechanic, living in Christchurch. And my youngest brother Graeme won't be there. He keeps himself to himself. You'll meet him at the pub sometime."

15

"Cabin crew, take your seats for landing."

The butterflies in my stomach flapped faster than hummingbirds in a David Attenborough documentary. I'd stored up an important question which I needed to ask before I met Fiona's parents.

3. DEATH'S CORNER

I took a deep breath.

"D'you think your dad would let me work on the farm? I'd love to learn how to milk cows."

"I'm not sure he'll allow you to milk. That's a job for the professionals. They'll find something for you to do, though."

Fiona paused.

"I should warn you, folks in my hometown don't have a high opinion of city dwellers. They believe people who live in places like London spend their lives driving fancy cars and eating at posh restaurants, and that they don't have a clue about the countryside or where their food originates. Some locals might call you a 'townie' or a 'pen-pusher'."

She gritted her teeth, sucked in a breath, and put her hand on her chin. "D'you think you'll be okay with that?"

"I don't want to be thought of as a pen-pusher. I want to fit in. I'm determined to learn the country ways."

"Good for you," said Fiona. "I'm not keen on farming, but I was born here, so nobody calls me a townie."

A small lady with short, brown hair, accompanied by a teenage girl embraced Fiona in a family huddle. I gripped the luggage trolley and hung back from the reunion. They broke apart. I rubbed my hands together and bit my lip.

Fiona pulled me forward.

"Simon, this is my mum, Linda."

Linda's sun-weathered cheeks demonstrated a country life spent outdoors. I reckoned she'd applied her lipstick in the car, possibly without the benefit of a mirror.

"Hello, Simon. I finally meet the boy who swept my daughter off her feet. Welcome to New Zealand."

"Thanks, Linda. And thank you for having me."

Angela grinned. She flicked her blonde hair over her shoulder and rested her hands on her hips, like Cindy Crawford on a Vogue cover. "Here's the city boy," she said. "Have you ever seen a cow?"

"One or two." I raised my eyebrows, nodded, and smiled. "Mainly dead ones in the supermarket."

"Leave him alone," said Linda. "They have cows in England."

Linda and Fiona discussed the health of relatives while Angela masticated chewing gum. I wrestled with the luggage trolley, which enjoyed a more scenic route across the car park than I had intended.

Angela opened the front passenger door.

"No, you don't," said Linda. "You rode in the front on the way here. And your sister feels sick going over the mountains."

Angela glared at Fiona and sauntered around the bonnet.

I slipped into the rear seat next to the hand luggage. Angela sat on the other side and folded her arms.

"Bloody city traffic," said Linda, as we queued behind a solitary car. We pulled on to the main road, and she began a presentation for Fiona's benefit, specifying who in their home town had married, which couples lived together, who'd died, and who'd moved away. I drew a mental Venn diagram as Linda explained some people who'd married had also moved away, some people who'd moved away were now dead, and some people hadn't moved away or died, but lived with different partners than the ones they were currently married to.

We passed a McDonald's, and the outer suburbs of Christchurch gave way to a quilt of green-and-brown countryside. Mailboxes sentried at the end of gravel driveways, and road signs indicated astronomical distances to unfamiliar locations.

"Where do all the sheep live, Linda?" I asked.

"What sheep?"

"All the New Zealand sheep. Everyone knows New Zealand's full of sheep."

"I'm not sure where you heard that. It's primarily cows where we are."

Through the windscreen, I gazed at the view of the snow-capped peaks, which reminded me of the Swiss Alps. I anticipated the appearance of a herd of goats with flowers around their necks, shepherded by a sweet, curly-haired, little girl.

"What's the range of mountains called, Linda?"

"The Alps," she replied.

Linda changed down a gear, and we entered the foothills.

The front seat conversation petered out.

Left bend.

Up.

Right bend.

Up.

Linda pointed to an outcrop of factory-sized boulders scattered across undulating, green slopes. "Castle Hill," she said. "It's a popular spot for tramping."

What's tramping? I need to learn these New Zealand expressions.

I peered over Fiona's shoulder. "Why have we stopped?"

"It's a one-lane bridge," she said. "Something's coming the other way."

I grabbed her headrest and pulled myself forward.

"A one-lane bridge? Isn't this the main road to the West Coast?"

A truck rumbled towards us across a span barely wide enough to contain its girth.

It towed two trailers, and the road vibrated like a washing machine on a spin cycle. The driver waved, and I read 'Trans-West Freighters' on the trailers' sides.

"Ready for the sex bridge, Simon?" asked Angela. She giggled.

My cheeks flushed.

"I beg your pardon? Sex bridge?"

"You'll see what she means," said Fiona.

Linda pulled away, and we traversed the long span over a grey-ribbon river.

Boing.

I bounced in my seat.

Boing.

Linda sped up.

Boing, boing, boing,

19

Angela grinned and watched for my reaction.

Boing, boing, boing, boing, boing, boing, boing, boing, boing.

The ride ended, and the return to two-way asphalt provided post-coital recovery.

"That's why it's called the sex bridge," she said.

≈≈≈

"I should slow down," said Linda, as we entered the first sign of human habitation for over an hour. "The speed cops wait here."

"How much further is it?" I asked.

"About ninety minutes."

"Are you bored, with no traffic and skyscrapers to look at, city boy?" asked Angela.

"Wait 'til we reach the pass," said Fiona.

Splodges of colour-accessorised trees stretched up the mountain slopes. Their deep-red flowers and dark-green branches reminded me of a Liberty's Christmas display. I wondered if explorers had ever penetrated the dense forests.

I leant into the car door as we swung left.

I leant into the hand luggage as we swung right.

Tight left bend.

Tight right bend.

Left.

Right.

"Can we stop?" asked Fiona. "I feel sick."

"You always feel sick," said Angela.

Linda halted in a small, gravel car park. Fiona opened her door and sat with her head in her hands.

"Are you okay?" I asked.

"I'll recover in a minute. This always happens to me on the mountain roads."

I stepped out and inhaled cool, misty air. Linda tugged a jacket from the boot.

"Could I grab something, too?" I asked. I unzipped the top of a suitcase and retrieved a fleece.

"KEEEEE-AAAAAAAAAAARRR."

The hair on the back of my neck stood up. I froze, then turned around.

"KEEEEEEE-AAAAAAAAAAAAAAAAAARRR."

A plump, green ball of feathers waddled towards me, like a policeman on the beat with his hands behind his back.

I inspected the ball.

"Linda, is that a kiwi? My dad asked me to take a photo of one."

Linda laughed.

"You won't see a kiwi up here. It's a kea; a mountain parrot."

"Gosh, I thought parrots lived in tropical countries."

The kea's beak pierced a discarded salt and vinegar crisp packet. Finding the litter unsuited to the afternoon's dining experience, it lifted a claw, slid the packet off its mouth, and put its head on one side, to assess whether I might be endowed with anything more edible.

"Don't let it near the car," said Linda. She waved her arms. "Shoo, shoo." The kea flapped and landed a short distance away.

"Why don't you want it close to the car?" I asked.

"They're destructive buggers," said Linda. "They rip off windscreen wipers, and door seals."

The destructive bugger preened its feathers, launched, and alighted on an information board. It keeee-aarrrrred at me, to ensure I had correctly registered its change of address.

"How are you feeling, Fiona?" asked Linda.

"Better now I've breathed some fresh air."

"Shall we keep going?"

The gravel crunched as Linda drove out of the car park. We ascended a steep curve, and a sign welcomed us to Death's Corner. I had a mental image of a Monty Python hooded figure with a sickle, and I hoped he wasn't currently in residence.

"This is the summit, Simon," said Linda. "You're on the West Coast."

The West Coast.

The untamed, rugged West Coast.

I looked over my shoulder towards McDonald's and civilisation, swallowed hard, and stared through the windscreen.

The main West Coast road.

One lane.

A sheer cliff to my right.

A steep nose-dive into a raging torrent to my left.

"What happens if a car comes?" I asked. "Or one of those Trans-West trucks?"

"We give way," said Fiona. "They're ascending the mountain, so they must maintain momentum."

The road entered a concrete tunnel, fixed onto the mountainside.

"Landslips frequently closed the pass," said Linda, "so they built this shelter over the worst part."

"What causes the landslips?"

"Heavy rain. And earthquakes."

I stared at the tunnel's roof and hoped an earthquake would wait until we were clear.

≈≈≈

"You're listening to Scenicland FM news. Today, the president of Federated Farmers announced.."

"Sorry," said Linda, as she lowered the volume. "Frank always leaves the car radio turned up full."

"Are you awake, Simon?" said Fiona. "We're nearly home."

I sat up and winced.

Late afternoon sun glossed the sea between streaks of white cloud and the ruler-straight horizon.

No islands.

No boats.

Endless ocean.

Linda paused at a lattice of wooden beams, which spanned a narrow river.

A double-trailer tanker rumbled across, and I glimpsed the words 'Westland Dairy' logoed along its side.

"Linda," I said. "This one-lane bridge carries all the traffic in both directions, up and down the West Coast?"

"Yes."

"So, what on earth are these train tracks?"

4. A MIDNIGHT VISITOR

I sat up and stared, to ensure my eyes hadn't fooled me.

"What happens if the train comes? All the traffic, up and down the highway, and the railway as well, crosses this little, wooden, one-lane bridge. There must be accidents all the time."

"Calm down, city boy," said Angela. "There's one train a day. And there aren't many cars. This isn't London."

≈≈≈

The afternoon sun reflected on the mountains, as we diverged from the coast and headed inland. Herds of cows grazed in companies of calm; dots of black, white, and brown speckling the pool-table green fields.

A van passed, and Linda extended her index finger as she gripped the wheel. I noted the other driver echoed the gesture.

"Why d'you do that, Linda?" I asked. "With your finger."

"It's the West Coast salute; you give it to all the other drivers."

There's a whole etiquette around country living.

We rounded a bend, and a campervan approached.

I watched Linda's forefinger. She didn't extend it. Nor did the campervan driver.

"I thought you gave the West Coast salute to all the other drivers?"

"Not to loopies."

"What's a loopy?"

"Loopy's our word for tourists," said Fiona.

"Like you," said Angela.

I ignored her.

"Why are they called loopies?"

"Because when they travel around the South Island in their campervans, they do a big loop: down to Queenstown, up via the glaciers, and over Arthur's Pass back to Christchurch."

I reached up and grabbed the handle above the window as we bumped along a rough track, past endless, regimented fence posts connected with strands of silver wire.

Linda parked in front of a cream-and-pink wooden bungalow with a green, corrugated-iron roof.

"Welcome home, Fiona," said Linda. "And Simon, of course. Welcome to your new home."

I opened the car door and stretched. A brown-and-black cattle dog ran up and rubbed its head against my leg. I ruffled its pointy ears. It panted enthusiastically, and its tail polished the car's rear bumper.

"Hello," I said. "What's your name?"

"He's called Jazz," said Fiona. "He's the farm dog."

She stood astride him and scratched his sides. He rolled on his back, and she rubbed his tummy.

"Hey, Jazz," she said, "d'you remember me? I think you've got fatter since I last saw you."

Linda opened the car boot and pulled out a backpack. Fiona picked up a bag and lugged it into the house. Jazz trotted at her heels. Angela carried nothing.

I waited by the car and sucked in the anxiety of remoteness.

A twin-humped foothill behind the farm reminded me of a sleeping camel.

I raised my hand to my eyes and tried to discern where the pass bisected the mountains.

A horse's long, brown nose inspected me across a gate. I walked over and patted it. The horse jerked its head up and whinnied.

Fiona reappeared from the house. "What are you doing? Come inside, and I'll introduce you to Dad."

She lifted a small bag from the car and vanished again.

My tummy hummingbirds recommenced their complicated dance routine.

I reached into the boot for the final backpack.

I hoped we'd bought the right whisky.

The house door handle rotated both ways. I waggled it, but it wouldn't open.

"Where are you, Simon?" said Fiona's voice.

"By the door. I can't open it."

"Oh. We never use the front door. Come around the side. We always enter via the kitchen."

I dragged the bag up three steps to the kitchen door. A large tabby cat sitting on a table regarded me in horror and poured itself under a chair.

A pair of legs sat on a brown sofa next to a one-bar electric fire, and an open newspaper bracketed by two disconnected hands concealed the legs' owner.

I bit my nails.

"Fiona," I whispered, "pass me the whisky."

I waited near the kitchen door.

The newspaper lowered, revealing a man in his sixties with white tufts of hair and a ruddy face. His red-and-black checked shirt topped threadbare trousers, and he wore heavy socks with impressively sized holes. He fixated on a television in the corner, which transmitted bold, coloured text that meant nothing to me. The newspaper dropped on the floor, and he picked up a dented, silver radio with a bent aerial. We heard a click as he turned the left knob. The speaker broadcast static noise interspersed with truncated speech.

"I'll introduce you when this race finishes," whispered Fiona.

"… and it's Lady Seles in front, Lady Seles, followed by Tin Soldier. They're being chased by At Your Service coming up the outside. Lady Seles is losing the lead. Tin Soldier's going to place third. At Your Service passes Lady Seles on the outside. At Your Service has it, At Your Service by a head. What a result for Don and Shane Hayes. At Your Service takes first, followed by Lady Seles and in third place, Tin Soldier. The next race at Auckland will be…"

Fiona's father crumpled a small piece of paper, flung it in the fireplace, and turned the radio off.

"Pppfff," he said, "not such a great outcome today."

"Hi, Dad," said Fiona.

"Well," said her father, incorporating paragraphs of emphasis into a single word, "here's the prodigal daughter."

Fiona's father stood up. He wasn't any taller than when he was sitting. He hugged her.

"Dad, this is Simon."

I shuffled my feet.

This is it. Time to make a great first impression.

"Simon, is it? Pleased to meet you. I'm Frank."

He shook my hand. Despite his height, his palm engulfed mine. His skin felt rough, like a greengrocer's potato sack.

"So," he said, "you've ventured all the way from the big conurbation to familiarise yourself with the New Zealand experience?"

He uses a lot of long words. He must be very intelligent.

"Yes, thank you for having me to stay. I've brought you a gift."

I presented him the duty-free.

He pulled the whisky out of the box, twisted the bottle, read the label and grinned.

"Isn't that wonderful? Glenmorangie. My favourite."

He deposited the box by the television, next to four identical cartons.

"Come on, Simon," said Fiona, "I'll show you where we're going to sleep."

I picked up the backpack in two hands and hauled it through the kitchen to the rear of the house. Fiona opened a brown, wooden door and revealed a twin room, with single beds on either side of a two-drawer cupboard.

"Was this your room when you were a little girl?" I asked.

She picked up a Barbie doll and brushed her hand through its hair.

"Yep, I shared with Angela until my brothers left home."

"It's going to be cosy," I said, as I dumped the backpack between the beds.

"Dinner's ready," called Linda.

Linda set down five plates of pastry topped with white mush, topped with green mush.

I glanced at Fiona and back at the plate.

"Erm, what's this called?" I asked.

"Pea, pie and pudd," said Linda. "I didn't have time to make anything more complicated."

"Pea, pie and pudd," I repeated. "Yum. Err, what's in it?"

"Peas, pie and pudd," said Angela.

"Pudd?"

"Spud," said Fiona. "Potatoes."

She squirted half a bottle of Wattie's tomato sauce on her dinner. I copied her and forked up some pudd.

"Simon," said Linda, "d'you have many films of your travels to develop? I cut out this advert from the newspaper. It says you can send them to Auckland to be processed."

She handed me a newspaper clipping, which depicted an ecstatic man flaunting photographs of his attractive family.

"Um, thanks, Linda. I'm not sure about mailing them. We can't take the photos again if they're lost in the post. Is there anywhere else?"

"There's the chemist in town, but he might be more expensive."

Frank entered, carrying a half-full bottle of whisky and two glasses. He stood the tumblers in front of me, sat down, and poured a large splash into both.

"Here's a little drink to welcome you," he said. "Cheers."

He chinked his glass against mine. I raised the whisky to my lips and tested a sip.

"How d'you like that?" he asked.

"Very nice," I said, untruthfully.

"It's a delectable drop, Glenmorangie. It'll be wonderful to have another whisky drinker in the house."

I swallowed another molecule. I didn't want to drink it too quickly, in case he topped me up.

Fiona cleared plates.

I yawned and stretched.

"It's amazing to think we were in Tonga this morning," I said. "It seems weeks ago."

"I think we'll turn in," said Fiona. "It's been a massive day. See you in the morning."

I undressed, stepped over the backpack, and slid between the covers. I couldn't recall the last time I'd slept in a single bed. A teddy inspected me from the top of a dresser, and pictures suitable for an eight-year-old girl hung on the walls.

I blew Fiona a kiss.

"Your parents are very welcoming," I said. "Your dad uses a lot of long words. I hope I can understand them all."

"Wait until he tries to explain how to do something. Every other word's 'thingamy' or 'whatsernames'. I don't know how he gets his point across."

She switched off the bedside light.

I lay awake on my back.

I perceived the outline of the teddy in the moonlight.

Her little girl memories. My girlfriend's childhood. I've still got so much to learn about her.

≈≈≈

I was in the middle of a disturbing nightmare, where Frank had challenged me to a whisky drinking competition. He topped me up again and again, but no matter how much I consumed, the level of liquid in the bottle never dropped, and four other bottles lined up waiting for our attention.

BOOOOM-BOOM-BOOOOOM

DRRRRRRRRRRRRRRRRRRRRRRRRRRRRRRR

RUMBLE RUMBLE RUMBLE

The house shook. I gripped the sides of the bed and sat up.

What happened? Was that an earthquake? Should we evacuate?

Clock.

Midnight.

I reached up and pulled the curtain to one side. Thousands of stars pin-pricked a sky as black as an undertaker's coat, and I distinguished trees silhouetted against their light.

Did I dream that noise?

Fiona slept.

No-one else stirred.

I crept out of the bedroom, walked into the lounge, and peered out of the window.

Across the farmyard I saw truck headlights and a man standing in front of them.

I narrowed my eyes, opened the kitchen door a crack and peeked out.

The starlight reflected in Jazz's water bowl.

His head rested on his paws. He raised his eyebrows and wagged the tip of his tail.

You're not much of a guard dog, are you?

The man entered one of the farm buildings.

The headlights illuminated his legs. He carried a box with a handle.

I have to raise the alarm. But I can't go into Frank's bedroom; I've only met him today.

I closed the kitchen door, strode to our bedroom, and shook Fiona.

She turned over. "What do you want? Go back to sleep. It's the middle of the night."

"There's a man in the farm with a truck. He's broken into a shed. He's stealing something. We need to wake your dad."

---

5. THE SCENICLAND RADIO

"Fiona, get up. We have to tell your dad about the burglar."

"For goodness sake, it'll be the tanker driver collecting yesterday's milk. Go back to bed."

She turned over and pulled up her covers.

I stood in the dark.

The tanker driver.

The milk collector.

I've got so much to learn.

I heard the tanker rumble back down the gravel drive.

Silence.

I climbed into bed, lay awake, and gazed at the ceiling.

I'm with Fiona.

My girlfriend.

In remote, rural New Zealand. Where earthquakes cause landslips, trains run over one-lane bridges, and suspicious milk tankers storm past in the middle of the night.

I'm a long way from McDonald's.

Crunch... scrunch... scrunch... crunch...

A river of black-and-white animals trudged along a track outside my window. Steam puffed from their nostrils like a procession of four-legged teapots.

A slow smile built on my face.

Fiona slept. I tugged on clothes, gingerly turned the doorknob, and tiptoed out.

A continual industrial hum emanated from the building where the suspicious tanker man had been engaged in his nocturnal activities.

Jazz jumped up, shook himself, and followed me across the farmyard.

I hesitated outside the shed.

Am I allowed in here?

I breathed in through my nose.

A strong, not unpleasant scent of hot farm animal.

A whiff of black rubber, which reminded me of changing a flat tyre.

A sharp, chemical smell I couldn't identify.

I stood near the entrance and strained to understand conversation.

"..thanks to Patricia on the news desk. Today's weather will be a perfect West Coast day; eighteen degrees and wall-to-wall sunshine. This is 93.1 Scenicland FM; thank you for joining us this morning. The time is 6:40. And now 'Broken Wings' by Mr Mister."

I poked my nose into the shed and observed Frank standing in a lowered concrete trench, between two rows of cows' bottoms. He yanked long, black hoses from the cows' undersides, hung them up, and squirted liquid from a squat, plastic bottle.

I edged around the corner.

Another taller man sprayed paint on a cow's back. I grimaced as her tail lifted, and she distributed a stream of light brown liquid, like a chocolate fountain when you stick your finger into the flow. The man spurted water from a thin hose and rinsed the liquid into a grate.

At the opposite end of the shed, a herd of cows waited in a concrete yard. They jostled and mooed as they queued for their turn to milk, and their noise added an interesting descant to the radio music.

Frank noticed me.

"Morning, Simon," he shouted above the cacophony. "Did you sleep well?"

I decided not to mention the midnight tanker.

"Fine, thank you."

I stepped into the trench, and the taller man held out his hand.

"Simon, is it? I'm Phillip, Fiona's brother."

He grinned behind his Burt Reynolds moustache.

"Hi Phillip," I said. "Nice to meet you. I arrived yesterday."

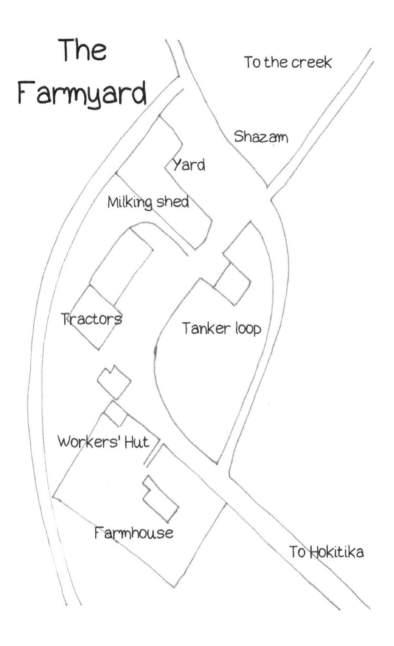

The Farmyard

To the creek

Shazam

Yard

Milking shed

Tractors

Tanker loop

Workers' Hut

Farmhouse

To Hokitika

"Phillip runs the farm," said Frank. "I'm his assistant these days. D'you want to watch what happens here? I don't suppose you'll have seen an operation like this in London."

Phillip strode along the walkway, his shorts and Wellington boots poking around the edge of a knee-length apron. He watched egg-shaped glass windows embedded in the black hoses and knew precisely at which stage each cow was in the milking process. His brisk, deft actions attached the milking tubes to the cows one by one. Frank removed them, squirted the udders with ochre liquid, opened a metal gate, and the row of cows departed. He clanged it shut, like a scene from *The Shawshank Redemption*. The next cows lined up, and Phillip marched along the row of new customers, flicking the black tubes on to each udder with practised wrist movements.

I crossed my arms and watched from the end of the channel, out of the tail-lift target zone.

Everyone involved enacted this routine daily.

Frank and Phillip could milk the cows without thinking about it.

The cows knew what the farmers expected of them.

This is not my world. I feel stupid in my fashionable jeans and branded T-shirt.

Frank read my mind.

"Find some farming clothes, Simon. You don't want to get those ones filthy. There'll be something in the storeroom."

Frank's old trousers and yellow Massey Ferguson Tractors-branded jumper smelt of cow. My thumb tugged the gap which betrayed the difference in our girth, and I threaded a piece of orange twine through the belt loops.

Jazz looked up at me and put his head on one side. He sniffed my knee and seemed to approve of my new attire.

I fidgeted at the end of the shed.

Phillip grinned. "What d'you reckon, Simon? The best thing about this job is that you get to feel eight hundred tits every day."

I chuckled.

I don't want to sound naïve. They might call me a townie.

I took a deep breath.

"Phillip, how many cows d'you milk at once?"

"Twenty-four. This shed's called a herringbone. There are twelve cows each side, and we stand in the middle to reach their udders."

One cow raised her tail. Phillip grabbed my arm and pulled me aside. Browny-green cow muck spattered on the concrete, and Phillip pointed the hose and washed it away.

Oh no. He thinks I'm worried about getting dirty.

"Is milking always a two-person job?" I asked.

"I can do it by myself if there's no-one around, but it's a lot easier with two. Frank gives me a hand."

Frank opened the gates one at a time. Twelve cows walked out each side, and the next customers entered.

"Why do the cows have a yellow tag in their ear?"

"Each tag has a number. We keep a record of the cow's milking and calving history, their health record, and their ancestry."

I imagined a parchment family tree with a bull's head displayed on a red-and-gold crest at the top.

"Why do some cows have orange colour on their backs, Phillip?"

"We spray their tails with this." He showed me an aerosol can. "If the paint's rubbed off, we can tell the bull's mounted them, and they should be pregnant."

Phillip pressed the top of the aerosol and squirted Jazz's tail to demonstrate. The dog put his head on one side. He didn't seem to mind.

I watched Frank remove the milking machine from each udder and spray the ochre liquid like Lynx underarm deodorant.

"Frank, what's in the spray?"

"It's disinfectant," he said. "It helps prevent mastitis."

"What's mastitis?"

I'd better slow down with the questions.

"It's an udder infection. If a cow suffers from it, we have to administer antibiotics. We can't include her milk in the day's production as it's not human-grade."

I scraped my hand through my hair.

"Frank, is there anything I could do to help? I want to learn how all this works."

Frank laughed.

"All right, stand up by the thingamy. The gate. When I put my thumb up, pull the whatsernames and release the twelve completed cows. Don't let any more through; some of them are keen to dash for fresh grass before we've milked them."

I stepped out of the trench, stood at the gate, and wiggled the metal bolt to ensure I could open it. The pressure of the front cow against the bars pushed against my hand. I stared at Frank and watched for his signal.

Phillip removed the milking machine from the cows' udders. They didn't finish giving milk in the same sequence they'd started, and I made a mental note to ask him about this.

I wiggled the bolt again. It still moved.

I watched Frank squirt each udder with his spray bottle. He turned, smiled, and gave me a thumbs-up.

I drew the bolt back and unlatched the gate. I expected to be trampled by a stampede, like one of the more exciting scenes in a Clint Eastwood movie.

The cows strolled out in a slow and gentle procession. Their heads nodded as they walked.

Five, six, seven,

One cow hesitated. Phillip slapped its bottom.

Eight, nine, ten,

Indistinguishable animals. Big and black-and-white, each with her own yellow ancestral ear-tag.

Frank watched me.

Jazz lapped at a puddle of spilt milk.

Oh, no. Was that eleven or twelve?

6. SHAZAM

I hesitated and raised my eyebrows. Frank's hand made a stop sign, I slammed the gate, and slid the bolt. The next cows walked up, and Phillip attached the milking machines.

I beamed, and he smiled at my relief I'd completed my task. *First initiative test passed.*

≈≈≈

Linda pulled packets of cereal from a cupboard above her head.

"Help yourself, Simon. The milk's in the fridge."

I sat at the table with a bowl of Nutrigrain.

Frank entered and pushed a blue plastic bottle into the rubbish. He wiped his hands on a tea-towel.

Linda inspected the bin.

"Frank," she said, "with all the soap products in the laundry, why did you wash your hands with Comfort fabric softener?"

He winked at me and placed two Weet-bix in a bowl.

I'll wait until he sits down before I ask any more questions. I hope his explanations aren't too complicated.

Frank picked up yesterday's newspaper, sat at the table, put on a pair of glasses, and opened it at the racing pages.

"Don't be rude," said Linda. "Put that away."

Frank smiled at me and shrugged. He folded the paper and lay it at the end of the table.

I swallowed some Nutrigrain.

"Frank, how much milk does each cow produce?"

"Our cows are Holstein-Friesians," said Frank. "They can give up to fifty litres a day. Some farmers keep the smaller light-brown Jersey cows. They don't provide such large quantities, but their milk's creamier."

He spooned Weet-Bix into his mouth.

"What happens to the milk when the tanker takes it away?"

"It's transported to the factory in town, where it's manufactured into baby formula and butter for export. You must have seen it on the supermarket shelves in London."

I tried to remember the layout of Sainsbury's dairy aisle. I wasn't sure of the colour of Frank's butter packaging.

"How do the cows know which way to walk once you let them out of the shed?"

Frank and Linda both laughed.

I put my head down and shovelled in a spoonful of cereal. Frank wiped his mouth with his hand.

"Sorry, Frank," I said. "Was that a silly question?"

"Of course not. Although, I've never heard anyone ask it before."

You've never had a city boy to stay before.

"We leave the gates shut along the track so there's only one way the cows can walk," said Frank. "Some of the older animals take the lead; they're the matriarchs, and the rest of the herd follows them to the fresh pasture."

"Okay, so you leave the gate open to the field they're headed for, and it's like a maze with one exit; they follow the tracks."

"Erm, yes. I suppose you could express it that way. I'll show you after breakfast. You could assist me with the gates for this evening's milking, if you're interested."

"Of course, Frank." I grinned and nodded my head. "Anything to help."

"There's one regulation on the farm," said Frank. He put down his spoon, his mouth straightened, and he stared at me. "If a gate's open, leave it open; if a gate's closed, leave it closed."

"Leave every gate as I find it. Understood."

Fiona entered the room dressed in her pyjamas. She noticed my Massey Ferguson jumper and grinned.

"Have you been milking the cows, Simon? Not too scary for you?"

"He's been helpful," said Frank. "Amazing, for a boy from London. I didn't think he'd want to get his hands messy."

"I'm helping Frank set the gates after breakfast," I said to Fiona.

My chest swelled, and I anticipated her reaction.

"Rather you than me," she said.

"Fiona's not a fan of cows," said Linda, "they're a bit big for her." She picked up a pen and began writing a list on a small piece of paper. "Would you two like to come into town this afternoon? I need to pick up some groceries. That is, Simon, if Frank can spare you."

Frank pushed himself up and put two slices of bread in a toaster.

He smiled and nodded. "I think we'll manage."

Everyone laughed.

The city boy was proving to be a source of great amusement.

≈ ≈ ≈

Frank sat astride a dark-green, four-wheel motorbike with a bright-blue, square, plastic bucket fixed to its front. Jazz jumped on to the bike and balanced on a shelf behind him. I noticed pebbles lodged in the tyres' knobbly bits.

"This is the primary vehicle we use to travel around the farm," said Frank. "Hop on." He patted the mudguard twice, and I sat on it. The bike throbbed as he turned a key.

Jazz licked my ear. I wiped it with my sleeve and rubbed his head.

Frank pulled a small, black lever.

My bottom vibrated as if I were sitting on a pneumatic drill, and I held on to Jazz with my right arm. We crossed the farmyard, drove past the milking shed and entered a track. I breathed in through my nose, as unfamiliar fragrances of animals, grass and salt air filled my nostrils.

A loud *click-click-click-click* bothered me.

"Frank, what's the clicking noise?"

"It's the electric fence short-circuiting. If the fences touch wet grass they click."

"How powerful are the fences?" I asked.

"Eight thousand volts."

"Pardon? Eight thousand volts?"

I recalled a rather graphic information film shown at my school, entitled *Charley the Cat says Don't Climb Pylons*. A scene entered my mind, where an unconscious teenager lay on the ground surrounded by paramedics.

"Doesn't that voltage hurt the cows?" I asked.

"It's only a 120-milliampere current," said Frank. "It's similar to a bee sting. They know to keep away."

I gasped as a rhinoceros-sized cow leant over a fence and inspected me.

"That's Shazam," said Frank. "He's a breeding bull, and the most valuable animal on the farm."

The most valuable animal on the farm stuck its long tongue out, curled it up, and inserted it into one nostril. I attempted to replicate this achievement without success.

"How much land d'you own, Frank?"

"Six hundred acres," he said. He pointed to the two-humped hill behind us. "The farm extends close to Camelback mountain and to the river at the end of this track."

"How many animals d'you keep?"

"Depends on the time of year. At calving time there are lots. Right now we're milking 205 cows, and we're feeding over two hundred beef cattle. Oh, and three horses."

"What are the horses for? D'you ride them on the farm?"

I had a vision of myself dressed as John Wayne, careering across the countryside on a white charger, lassooing escaped bulls.

Frank laughed. "We don't ride them. I breed them for racing; it's a hobby of mine. There's twelve in total. Three here, and nine away with trainers in Christchurch."

Twelve racehorses? Am I dating a racing heiress?

I studied Frank's woolly checked shirt and stained trousers and decided racehorse owning must be more common in New Zealand.

Frank edged the bike down the bank of a knee-deep stream. I watched long, green river weed bow down in the glass-clear water. Ruts showed where generations of farm vehicles had exited.

"Are we going through the water?" I asked.

Frank laughed. "It's the only way to cross it. We call this 'the creek'. We'll arrive at the main Hokitika River on the other side."

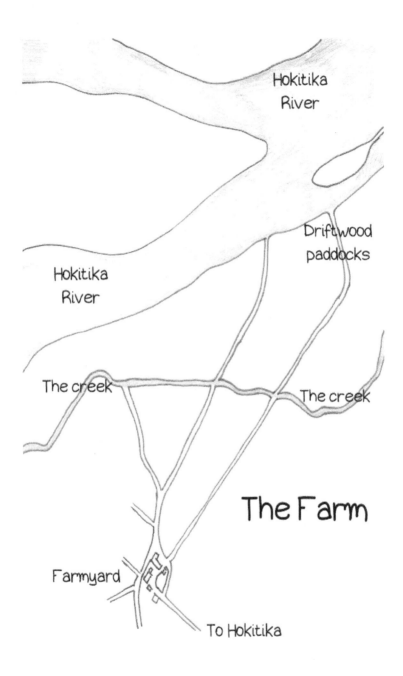

The creek washed the bike's wheels. I lifted my feet. Frank accelerated up the bank, stopped at a gate, and turned off the bike. I rubbed my hands together, as the twinges of being a long way from civilization increased.

Remote.

Silent.

Desolate.

I stood on tiptoes to ensure I could still see the farm buildings behind us.

A wide river flowed past meadows strewn with dead branches, as if an angry giant had uprooted trees and thrown them around the fields.

"What happened, Frank? Why is all this wood lying here?"

"Flood," said Frank. "When it rains hard, the river floods, merges with the creek, and inundates these paddocks. The water's so powerful that trees rip out of the banks, float downstream, and terminate their journey here."

"Does that happen often?"

"Once or twice a year. Then someone has the job of clearing it away."

"That's something I could do to help," I said. "It sounds easier than milking."

Jazz barked at a rabbit. Its white tail vanished under a gorse bush.

Frank undid a small chain, opened a gate, and hooked up a spring-loaded electric fence. This blocked the track, and I could see it would divert the cows to their evening pasture.

"We graze the cows this side of the creek when it's dry," he said. "These paddocks next to the river can become swampy."

Frank looked at me.

"Would you like to drive the bike back to the farm?" he asked.

I blew out a long breath and smiled.

"Really? Through the creek?"

"Keep your engine revs up," said Frank. "That way, water won't enter the whatsernames."

I sat astride the bike. Jazz hopped on the tray, and Frank occupied my previous position on the mudguard.

"Oh, and remember not to change gear in the middle of the creek," he said.

"I've no idea how to change gear at all."

"You push this pedal with your foot and pull the thingamy."

"Thingamy?"

"Here," said Frank. He put my hand on the right handle grip and pressed my fingers on a small lever. The engine noise increased.

I furrowed my brow.

"Squeeze it," said Frank.

I squeezed.

The bike crept forward.

"A bit faster," said Frank.

I pulled the throttle involuntarily every time we drove over a bump. Frank sat on the side with his mouth in a straight line.

"Let the bike roll into the creek," he said. "Once the front wheels touch the water, pull on the whatsernames again."

"I could do with L-plates."

I braked. Driving a vehicle into a stream didn't feel natural.

The front wheels entered the water.

I remembered Frank's instructions and pulled on the whatsernames.

A tsunami surged in front of the bike.

"Slow down," said Frank.

We reached the opposite bank. I pushed my shoulders back and sped up.

Second initiative test passed.

I stopped the bike outside the farmhouse, kicked off my boots, and ran indoors.

"Fiona, guess what. I drove the four-wheel bike through the creek."

"You'll be a farmer in no time," she said.

Frank followed me. He grinned at my enthusiasm.

"Afternoon milking's at 3:30, Simon. If you return from town in time, you could come with me and fetch the cows."

"Wow. Yes, please," I said. "I'd love to help."

43

The unfamiliar names of assorted cough and cold remedies on the chemist's display interested me, as I waited for him to serve his previous customer.

I picked up a scented candle, opened the lid, and recoiled.

"May I help you?"

The pharmacist leant on the counter and inspected me over his glasses.

I replaced the candle.

"D'you develop camera films?"

His bald head shone under the store lights, and his white coat displayed blue streaks where his ball-point pen had missed his top pocket.

"The very best quality prints," he said, sounding like a well-rehearsed radio advertisement. "Developed using Kodak Gold technology."

"Great, I've twenty 36-picture films plus three disposable cameras. There's a company in Auckland advertising in the local newspaper. I wondered if you could match the price?"

I offered him the cutting of the cheerful man with his family photos.

The chemist held it at arm's length between his thumb and forefinger, as if I'd handed him a particularly explicit *Playboy* centrefold. He grimaced and clenched his teeth.

He placed it to one side. I wondered if he was going to wash his hands.

The cash register beeped.

"Twenty 36-picture films plus three 24-picture disposable cameras. That'll be five hundred and sixty dollars, please."

My eyebrows raised.

"Five hundred and sixty dollars?"

Has he put the decimal point in the wrong place?

"Five hundred and sixty dollars," he said. "Twenty-five dollars each for the 36s, and twenty dollars for the 24s."

I stared and shook my head. "It's only £2.99 per film at the newsagent's in London."

"Develop them in London, then. That's the price here."

"What about the newspaper offer?"

"I wouldn't bother," he said, "those companies are rip-offs. The quality won't be any good."

44

I handed him a quarter of all the money I owned; the register opened and consumed my life savings.

"The photos come back in a week," said the chemist.

"A week? You don't develop them here?"

"No, they're sent to Auckland. Anything else you need?"

I wondered if they were processed by the company advertised by the ecstatic man with the beautiful family.

"Erm, no, thanks. I'll collect them in a week."

I perched on a bench outside a library to wait for Fiona and Linda and pulled the guidebook from my bag.

Hokitika, it explained, had been built one hundred and fifty years previously. Gold brought miners and their followers, and a shanty town sprung up. At one point, Hokitika boasted over one hundred pubs.

I gazed down the main street past the chemist's shop and tried to imagine how life might have been in Victorian days.

I'm a poor labourer, and I've come to Hokitika to dig for gold. Pounds and pounds of gold. A man in a pub back home in Dublin told me about fortunes to be made in a little town in New Zealand. All I've brought with me are my clothes and a few simple tools. I'm going to stake a claim up a secret river I've heard about and become a wealthy man. But first, after my long journey, I need a beer in one of these pubs.

"Hello," said a lady I'd never seen before in my life. "You must be Simon."

7. HOKEY POKEY

The lady grasped a four-wheeled trolley with a red-and-brown tartan exterior.

I tried to determine where she could have known me from.

"Err, yes, I'm Simon."

She detached her glasses and examined me.

"We've heard about you," she said, "coming all the way from the big city. What do you think of our little town?"

"Very nice. Lovely part of the world."

"I don't know how you townies manage with all the pollution and smog. And it's so expensive; how do any of you afford to live in London?"

I considered explaining film developing was substantially cheaper.

"I couldn't live anywhere like that," she said. "Hokitika, best place in the world."

"Have you lived here long?" I asked.

"Born and bred. Wouldn't live anywhere else."

I began to feel inadequate for not being raised in Hokitika.

"I must go," she said. "Nice to meet you."

The lady trundled her trolley away, leaving me with no idea of who she was, or how she knew my name.

Two more ladies passed. They waved and smiled. I hesitated and waved back.

Fiona and Linda strolled up to me.

"Have you coped by yourself?" said Fiona. "D'you want to come to the supermarket?"

"Fiona," called Linda, across the four short aisles that constituted the entire store, "could you grab some Tip Top?"

"Tip Top," I said. "What's Tip Top?"

"Have you ever tried hokey pokey?" Fiona asked me.

"Hokey cokey?"

"Tip Top hokey pokey ice cream," said Fiona. "You can't buy it in England."

"I've never heard of it."

She reached into a chest freezer and extracted a square tub with a picture of a scoop of brown-and-cream dessert in a white bowl. She added it to the trolley.

"I'll just go to the back of the store and choose some Tip Top."

"I thought we bought the Tip Top," I said. "The ice cream."

"I mean bread. It's also called Tip Top."

Linda loitered in the middle of an aisle. She chatted with another lady. Their trolleys stood side by side and obstructed all other shoppers' purchasing activities.

"Simon, this is Beryl," said Linda. "She lives up the valley. She farms deer."

Beryl smiled from her ruddy red face. Her hair poked upwards and sideways, as if someone had yanked her out of bed and immediately shoved her through a gorse bush.

Try to appear knowledgeable, Simon.

"Pleased to meet you, Beryl," I said. "How many deer d'you milk on your farm?"

Beryl laughed out loud and covered her mouth. Linda clenched her teeth and giggled.

I felt my cheeks ripen and looked at my shoes.

"We don't milk them," said Beryl. "We keep them for meat. It's called venison."

She grinned at me. "Linda says you're keen on farming. You can visit our farm if you're interested."

"Thanks," I said, "I could do with the education."

Fiona dropped three transparent bags of bread in the trolley. "I found a new Tip Top flavour," she said. "Cranberry and coconut."

"Cranberry and coconut?" I said. "Wow. What happened to brown, white, and wholemeal?"

Linda glanced at her watch.

"We'd better go home. The men will want their dinner."

I leant, forward in the car's front seat to examine trains of cows walking from their milking sheds, their heads nodding rhythmically. Some were black-and-white Friesians like Frank's, some were smaller brown Jerseys, and some were mixed-up combinations of the two.

Linda clicked the boot and unloaded groceries. I pulled on my Massey Ferguson jumper and ran to the shed, as Frank released the last cow from the gate and the hum of the milking machine ceased. Phillip kick-started a two-wheel motorbike, waved to me, and followed the line of cows.

"Evening, Simon," said Frank. "You've missed milking."

I frowned and kicked a stone.

"Sorry, I met several people in town. Is there anything I could help with now?"

"You could wash the yard. I'll show you how."

"Of course. Whatever you need."

A thick layer of cow muck covered the concrete like chocolate rice-pudding; the product of 205 cows lingering for their turn to be milked.

Frank picked up a white hose as round as his forearm. He turned a tap, and a Niagara of water smashed onto the concrete floor.

"Direct it so the muck washes down the whatsernames and through the hole in the side of the yard."

Another new skill. I'm becoming more useful.

I pointed the hose at the ground. Some of the muck shifted, but the afternoon sun had baked the lower layers hard at gas mark eight, and the dirt stuck to the concrete.

If you require more pressure, stick your hand down the pipe," said Frank. "I'll show you."

He took the hose from me and bent four fingers in the end.

The water gushed, and the muck oozed like a volcano's lava flow.

He handed me the hose.

I copied him. Water squirted backward and soaked me.

Frank grinned. "I'll leave you to practise."

≈≈≈

Frank, Angela, and Fiona sat at the dining table, as I kicked off my boots and entered. Frank inspected the racing pages, folded the newspaper, and rested it on top of a library of previous editions.

"Something smells good," I said. "What's for dinner tonight?"

"Steak," said Linda. She placed plates of meat and potatoes in front of us and sat down.

I contemplated the steak.

I gazed out of the window at a group of black-and-white calves. They gambolled in the evening sun and seemed happy.

I tried not to connect the two and picked up my knife and fork.

"Nolene said she spoke to you in town, Simon," said Linda.

"She did?"

"Yes. She saw you sitting on the bench outside the library."

"But how did she know me?"

"Oh, everyone will know who you are. It's not London."

I chewed my steak.

"It's going to be glorious weather for the next two days," said Linda. "Are you three kids keen to go tramping up the Fox River?"

My forehead wrinkled.

Tramping. There's that word again.

"We could stay in the ballroom overnight," said Angela.

"Ballroom?"

I had a vision of a BBC period drama, with powder-wigged aristocrats wearing intricate masks, waltzing to a string quartet.

"Sounds fun," I said. "What do we need to take?"

"Bring your tent and sleeping bags," said Linda. "And pack some food and drink."

Ahh. Tramping means camping. But what's this about a ballroom?

"Will we see any wild kiwis?" I asked. "I've promised my dad I'd photograph one for him."

Linda laughed.

"We'll keep a lookout. You never know."

≈≈≈

The grey linen of morning mist extended over the paddocks. A horse whinnied in the field next to the house, above the constant hum of the milking machine.

I breathed in the wonderful anticipation of warm weather and hovered on the front step with our tent and backpack.

Linda reversed her car out of the garage. Fiona and Angela climbed in the back with a bag between them.

"Mum," said Angela, "I don't have any space. Fiona's taking up too much seat."

"Stop arguing," said Linda. "It's like having two primary school children again."

She sped up as we exited the farm, turned north in the town, and followed the coast. I stared at biblical seas crashing on the shore to our left.

"Does anyone swim at the beach?" I asked.

"Only if they want to die," said Linda. "Every summer some loopy gets into difficulties and has to be rescued. There are currents, and undertows, and it's freezing, too. I can't understand why anyone would want to bathe in it. What's wrong with the town pool?"

We paused at my old friend the road-rail bridge and waited for a milk tanker to cross. Linda extended her index finger to the driver. He returned the greeting.

I continued my inspection of the ocean, but couldn't see any ships.

"This is Greymouth," announced Linda. "It's the big smoke around here."

We passed through the big smoke in three minutes and continued along the coast road. Dramatic cliffs bordered black-sand beaches. The waves rolled in and out, in and out.

Linda slowed, as we entered a small settlement entirely occupied by campervans.

"Loopies," I said, knowledgeably.

"Yep," said Fiona, "this is where the pancake rocks are. It's a tourist attraction."

"What are pancake rocks?" I asked.

"They're rocks shaped like pancakes," said Angela.

The car veered right, and I braced myself as we bumped through potholes. We parked in a small, gravel semicircle surrounded by Jurassic Park jungle.

I stepped out, rubbed my hands together, and gazed at the impenetrable rainforest.

Exotic bird calls echoed among the trees, and I inhaled the wonderful smell of warm, wet, morning earth. I tilted my head and listened to the ripples of an unseen river.

"How far is it to the campsite?" I asked.

"About four hours' walk," said Linda. "We'll follow the river."

"Four hours' walk?" I said. "Four hours?"

Angela laughed. "You're such a townie."

Linda led us in a single file. My boots crunched on loose pebbles as the track became rockier and narrower. Trickling water dripped down moss-covered rocks, and I stared up at the straight trunks of tall ferns.

The path widened, and I strode to catch up with Angela.

"Have you ever been tramping in England?" she asked.

I leant my head towards her and lowered my voice.

"Angela, what's tramping, exactly?"

Angela laughed and called out, "Mum, Simon doesn't know what tramping is."

"This is tramping," said Linda. "It's what we're doing now."

"Oh," I said, "we call it hiking. I did some years ago in England. On school camp in a region called The Lake District. It's similar to this; I suppose the mountains aren't as high."

We turned a corner and eyed skyscraper cliffs covered in lush vegetation, bordering a wide, transparent, shallow stream. I listened to the burbling over the stones and brushed aside a kite-sized leaf leaning into the water.

I furrowed my brow, tapped my flat finger on my mouth, and looked around.

"Where do we go?" I asked. "The path's ended."

"It's time to get our feet wet," said Linda. She marched into the river and sploshed through the shallows.

Angela followed.

Fiona and I hesitated.

Angela turned around. "Come on, townies," she said.

We linked arms.

I tiptoed and failed to prevent water from entering my boots. The river became deeper, and I felt saturated socks mould around my feet. We squelched out and rediscovered the path.

A basketball-sized bird with bright green plumage regarded me from a branch. I pointed at it.

"Can we wait for a sec?" I asked. "I want to photograph this pigeon. All we see in London are boring grey ones."

"It's a Kereru," said Linda. "That's the Māori name."

The Kereru investigated me. It put its head on the other side to see if I looked any better that way up and fluffed its feathers.

"They're officially endangered," said Linda. "They used to be common, but introduced rats eat their eggs."

I snapped a picture of the Kereru. It relaxed and preened its feathers. Its World Wildlife Fund conservation status didn't cause it any concern.

The path traversed the river again, and I abandoned any hope of keeping my feet dry.

A small, brown bird poked amongst the undergrowth. Its neck jerked as if it were auditioning for a dinosaur movie.

I gasped. "Linda, is that a kiwi?"

"I shouldn't think so." She peered at it, as the bird pecked behind a small fern. "It's a weka. A Māori chicken."

The weka scuttled up the track and vanished into the bushes.

I heard a crash and a deep snort. Something rustled in the trees. Something considerably bigger than a chicken.

8. SKREEEE

A long, brown head poked out from behind a fern and exhaled like a halting Trans-West truck.

I wrinkled my nose.

"It's a horse," I said. "Someone's sprayed paint on it."

The horse stared at me, snorted again, and tore grass from the edge of the path. Written on the side was the word 'cow'.

"Linda, what's this horse doing here?"

She inspected it.

"Someone's turned it loose to feed," she said. "They'll come back and fetch it later."

"Okay, but why does it say 'cow'?"

"It's so hunters don't think it's a deer and shoot it. The owner's written 'cow' for a laugh. They could have written 'sheep'. Or 'elephant'."

I considered the likelihood of encountering a horse in a forest with 'elephant' graffitied across its flank and decided there were some aspects of life on New Zealand's West Coast I could never hope to understand.

We completed our third river crossing. I removed my socks and inspected flakes of white skin falling off my soles. I'd have walked barefoot if my soft city feet could have coped with the Lego-sharp stones.

Linda watched me rub my toes.

"Is it much further?" I asked.

"Just around the next corner." She pointed upstream. "No more wet shoes."

I winced as the backpack straps knifed into my shoulders, and I followed her into the jungle.

"This," said Linda, "is the ballroom. We'll camp here tonight."

I gazed up at a space under a rock overhang that could have comfortably accommodated a double-storey house.

"Here?" I asked. "Under this?"

"Yep."

I looked up again.

"But what if it collapses during the night?"

"We'll be dead," said Angela.

"Come on," said Fiona, "help me put up the tent."

"How are we going to fit four of us in our little tent?"

"We'll leave the backpacks outside," said Linda.

"But someone might steal them."

"You're such a city boy," said Angela. "We're four hours from the nearest human being. No-one's going to steal them."

Linda collected some large stones from the river's edge and arranged them in a circle.

I puckered my lips and studied her actions. She gathered dry twigs and leaves, deposited them in the middle of the circle, and lit them with a match.

A fire flared up. She added larger twigs. I picked up lumps of wood and positioned them on top.

The flames died, and smoke rose.

Linda removed my contribution.

"Not like that, Simon, those are too green. Fetch some dry ones."

She crouched down and puffed. The flames reignited.

I dragged a small, dead tree from a shallow cave at the back of the ballroom.

"Will this do?"

"Perfect." She stamped, snapped it, and formed a pile of firewood.

She took off her socks and hung them on a rock to dry. I copied her.

The fire burned, and we sat around it as if we were extras in an Abba video.

I surveyed the overhang above us and hoped the fire's heat wouldn't cause a geological reaction.

Fiona cooked sausages in a frying pan. She removed potato-shaped pieces of tin foil from her backpack and poked them into the fire.

"What are those?" I asked.

"Potatoes wrapped in tin foil. Camp jacket spuds."

"Nice. What did you bring for breakfast?"

"Some cornflakes, a packet of milk, the loaf of cranberry and coconut Tip Top, butter, and jam. We can toast the bread on the fire."

I slapped my arms at midge pin-pricks.

Linda produced a small tin kettle, filled it from the river, and shoved it in the flames.

"Tea, anyone?"

≈≈≈

I yawned and stretched.

We squished into the two-person tent, and I formed a Simon-shaped bulge along one side. Fiona curved against me.

I lay half-asleep and reflected on my present situation.

Four hours' walk from the nearest road.

Four hours' walk from the nearest house.

Four hours' walk from the nearest human.

A precipitous mountain pass between me and McDonald's.

I listened to the river tinkle over the stones. I reflected on how it flowed non-stop, night and day, even if no-one was present to hear it.

A night-bird's call.

I wonder if that's a kiwi?

Silence.

The bird called again.

Peace.

Dark.

Sleep.

"SKRRREEEEEEEEEEEEEEEEE."

I opened my eyes wide and jerked my head up. The hairs on the back of my neck stood on end.

"SKRRREEEEEEEEEEEEEEEEEEEEEEEEE."

Pause.

"SKREEEEEEEEEEEEEEEEEEEEEEEEEEEEEEEEEE."

"What the hell's that?" I asked.

"Possum," said a sleepy voice.

"Possum? What's a possum?"

How big are they? Are they carnivores? Do they eat people?

"SKRRREEEEEEEEEEEEEE," the possum continued.

I lay rigid. Cold sweat beaded on my forehead.

No-one else seems concerned. How can they sleep when we're about to be eaten by a possum?

Rustle, rustle, rustle, rustle.

Right outside the tent.

The possum's going to come in. It'll rip into the tent and kill us.

Rustle, rustle.

"SKREEEEEEEEEEEEEEEEEEEEE."

Rustle, rustle, rustle.

It's at the door of the tent.

Sweat ran down my back.

No-one stirred.

Black.

Dark.

Silent.

Where is it? Will it mount another attack? Has it gone to fetch reinforcements so they can eat all four of us?

Silence.

If I'm motionless, the possum will think there's no-one in the tent.

Still.

Rigid.

Don't move, Simon.

Someone farted.

I opened my eyes wide and clenched my teeth.

Sshh, the possum will hear.

I wiped the sweat off my forehead with my pyjama sleeve.

I stared upwards into the dark.

I listened to the water trickle across the pebbles.

Silent Night.
Still.
Silent.

≈ ≈ ≈

"Simon, wake up," called Fiona. "Breakfast time."

I rubbed my eyes and opened the tent flap.

Sparkly diamonds reflected from the river as it rippled.

I heard Linda and Angela's voices, and splashes of water.

Fiona stood outside the tent with no clothes on. I raised my eyebrows, then realised she was the only one of us who could appropriately be naked in front of everyone else.

"Are you coming for a wash in the river?" she asked.

I pressed my lips together and jerked my head sideways.

"Are they wearing anything?"

"Angela's dressed in her swimmers. I'm not sure about Mum."

"I'll hop in when you've all finished."

I sat in the tent and read the guidebook.

The Fox River, it explained, was named after William Fox, a gold prospector from Ireland. It cascaded through spectacular mountain ranges, subterranean passages, and caverns. Between dairy and beef farms, the rusty remains of one hundred years of gold and coal mining machinery were scattered over the land. Visitors were advised not to stray from marked paths to avoid falling down disused mineshafts.

I ruminated on how West Coasters lived their lives lurching between drowning on fatal shores, being flattened by trains on one-lane road-rail bridges, and plummeting down suicidal mines.

"Simon, you can come out now. Mum's decent."

I opened the tent door and blinked in the sunlight. Linda wore a different top. Her hair dripped over her shoulders. Angela exhibited a fluffy green towel wrapped around her.

I stripped down to yesterday's underwear and waded in.

My heart stopped.

I gasped and held my breath.

Fiona walked down the stony bank.

"Are you going under? I did."

57

I clenched my teeth. "It's… so…. cold.."

I pointed my arms above my head, dived, and surfaced. I took short, sharp breaths.

My feet hurt on the stones as I ran out, grabbed a towel, and rubbed myself.

I hopped from left to right on a patch of grass.

"How.. can.. water.. be.. that.. cold and not freeze?"

"The river runs down the valley from high in the mountains," said Fiona. She pointed up at the peaks. "It might originate in a glacier."

"I feel like I bathed in a glacier."

I wrapped the towel around me, returned to camp, and stood in an electric blanket of sunlight.

Linda crouched over the fire, and smoke rose.

I'd better let her know I'm enjoying myself.

"Morning Linda," I said. "It's incredible to wake up here knowing there are no people for miles. It's so beautiful and so remote. I've never been anywhere like it. I could become used to this."

Linda rummaged in the bottom of a backpack.

"Someone's been here during the night," she said. "Our loaf of bread's gone."

9. CLEARWATER REVIVAL

"The loaf of bread's gone?" I asked. "Did we drop it on the way up?"

"We didn't," said Angela. "I pulled it out of the backpack last night when I grabbed my wash bag."

"Did you put it back?" asked Linda.

"I think so."

We searched the camp.

We scouted around the fire and probed among the rocks under the ballroom overhang.

Nothing.

No bread.

Not a crust.

Something flapped in the branch of a tree.

I walked towards it.

A plastic bag.

With a Tip Top logo.

"Found it," I shouted. "At least, I've found the bag."

"Bloody hell," said Linda. "Possums."

The hair on my neck stood on end, as I relived the previous night's Alfred Hitchcock movie.

"Possums?"

"Possums stole the bread and partied with it," said Linda. "Now we've only got the cornflakes."

"Erm, these possums," I asked. "What do they look like?"

"Have you never seen a possum?" asked Angela.

"They're similar to squirrels," said Fiona.

"Bigger," said Linda. "More the size of large cats or small dogs."

"What do they eat?" I asked.

"Bread, it would appear. And anything else they can find."

"Are they vegetarian?"

"Yes," said Linda. "They're an introduced pest from Australia. They eat through tons of New Zealand's native bush every night. They're nocturnal. Evil-looking animals."

Evil-sounding animals too.

We sat and crunched our cornflakes, to the endless melodies of the percolating river.

≈≈≈

I crossed and uncrossed my arms.

Here goes. I have to ask this question at some point. Morning teatime's as good as any.

"Frank, d'you think I could try milking the cows? Doing what you do?"

"It's their livelihood," said Fiona, "they don't want you stuffing it up."

"Let's start slowly," said Frank. "How about you help me with the gate and the spray? We could progress to removing the milking cups once you've mastered those."

"Cups?"

"The ends of the whatsernames that we attach to the udders. They're called cups."

"How do I tell when the cow's finished milking?" I asked. "Phillip seems to know instinctively."

"It's easy, city boy," said Angela. "The cow'll turn around and say, "moo, I've finished now, please take the cups off.""

Fiona laughed. Linda set her jaw and glared at Angela. I inspected the tablecloth.

"I'll help you," said Frank, "and before this afternoon's milking d'you want to assist with something else?"

"Of course. Anything to lend a hand."

"You remember those paddocks out by the river?"

"The ones with the driftwood in them?"

"That's them. Could you take the four-wheel motorbike, gather as many of the smaller lumps of timber as you can, and tip them over the riverbank? There's a little trailer you can hook up to the bike."

"What, take the bike by myself?"

"Only needs one of us."

"Erm, no problem. I hope I remember how to drive through the creek."

≈≈≈

My Massey Ferguson clothes smelt of eau-de-stale cow.

I discovered an upside-down cup-shaped hook at the front of the trailer, which rested on a ball at the rear of the four-wheel bike.

Jazz jumped on the tray behind my seat. I grinned as we rode towards the creek, and I heard him pant behind my right ear. If prizes were awarded for the happiest New Zealand farming employees, Jazz and I would win joint first.

We ploughed through the water.

Jazz barked.

"Quiet, Jazz. What's all the noise about?"

I opened the paddock gate to start work and glanced back at the bike.

Something didn't look right.

I scratched my head.

Oh no. Where's the little trailer?

I retraced my steps and found the trailer half-submerged in the creek, with a bow-wave washing around it.

The power of the current surprised me, as I removed my boots and waded in up to my knees.

I pulled the trailer's front end, but it wouldn't budge.

My foot stood on a sharp stone, and I winced.

The bottom of my shorts turned deep-blue as they dipped under the water.

I leant against the trailer and pushed.

It rolled forward a few inches and back again.

I pushed again as hard as I could. The trailer semi-circled and toppled me over. The force of the water tumbled me onto my back. I pulled myself up on the trailer and caught my breath.

Jazz stood on the bank, his tongue out, his ears pricked, and his head on one side.

Time to fetch help, Simon.

61

I sped the bike back to the farm. My boots squelched as I reached the kitchen door, and I inverted them in a flower bed.

The door opened.

Angela gawked at the Creature from the Black Lagoon.

"What happened to you? Did you fancy a swim?"

Frank poked his head around the corner, planted his hands on his hips, and grinned.

I lowered my head and dripped on the step.

"I'm sorry. I don't know how it happened, but the little trailer detached from the bike and it's lying in the creek."

"You look like you've been lying in the creek," said Angela.

A scarf of river-weed slimed from my neck and plopped on the doormat.

"Get in the shower," said Linda. "And undress where you are. We won't watch."

I shed my saturated clothes and ran naked to the bathroom.

≈≈≈

Frank tugged his boots on.

"I should've explained how to secure the trailer hitch thingy," he said. "I suppose you haven't done that before?"

I admitted this particular activity had been omitted from my urban education.

"No harm done; you'll learn. Let's rescue the trailer."

Jazz jumped on the bike. I perched on the mudguard, put my arm around him, and he snuffled my hand. I rubbed his ears. I loved Jazz. He didn't call me a city boy or laugh at my mistakes.

Frank clanked a long chain into the bike's bucket, and we drove towards the creek.

What if the trailer's not there anymore? What if it's been swept into the river? I don't have enough money to buy Frank a new one.

The trailer lay in the centre of the creek where I'd drowned it. Water swirled around its wheels.

"Fancy another swim?" said Frank. He smiled and handed me the chain. "Loop the end around the front of the whatsernames."

"D'you mean the trailer?"

"Yes. The metal drawbar at the front."

I'm getting better at translating Frank-speak.

"Attach it with the thingamy. The shackle."

"What's a shackle?"

Frank demonstrated a piece of metal in a half loop, with a bolt that completed a circle.

I held the end of the chain, wallowed towards the trailer, and attached the shackle.

Frank revved the bike and pulled the trailer out of the creek. He yanked weeds from the axle.

I watched and rubbed my lips.

I hope this isn't the end of my farming career.

"It's all right," he said. "No damage done. I'll show you how to hook it up properly, so this occurrence doesn't eventuate again."

He hitched the trailer to the back of the bike and released a small lever. I heard a click, and he wobbled the drawbar up and down. The trailer remained attached.

Frank looked at his watch. "You could come back and remove the driftwood after lunch," he said. "We'd better go home. There's racing from Christchurch this afternoon."

He sat on the mudguard. "You can drive."

I reversed the bike and tried to perform a three-point-turn on the track, but the trailer jackknifed.

"Have you backed a trailer before, Simon?"

"I haven't. Clearly I need some practice."

We swapped spots. Frank wiggled the bike, and we motored back the way we'd come.

≈≈≈

"It's Christmas in two days," said Fiona. "What are we doing?"

Linda filled sandwiches with ham and salad and waitressed them to the dining table.

"We're having it here," she said. "Phillip and his family's coming, and your nana and pop."

"Will Nana be bringing a trifle?" asked Angela.

"I hope so," said Fiona. "Christmas in London hasn't been the same without one."

"She'll have made it already," said Linda, "and a spare one in case Pop eats it before they arrive."

"Do the cows have to be milked on Christmas day?" I asked.

Everyone laughed.

"Yep, city boy," said Angela. "No day off for you."

"You don't have to assist on Christmas day if you don't want to," said Frank. "I think Phillip and I can cope."

"I'd like to, Frank. I want to learn how to milk by myself."

"I'm still astounded a boy from the city doesn't mind getting his hands dirty."

"I appreciate your hospitality," I said to Frank, "I'd like to be involved in any way I can."

I stuffed my lunch down as fast as I could without choking to death, ran outside, and turned the key in the four-wheel bike.

Jazz lay in the sun with his head resting on his crossed paws.

"Here, Jazz!"

He jumped up, shook, and leapt on the bike's tray. We motored off with the little trailer bouncing along behind us.

I grinned as we headed up the track again. I turned around and eyed the dog. He grinned too. I heard his huff-huff-huff in my ear. Shazam the bull studied us as we zipped past.

We stopped at the creek. Jazz jumped off and lapped the water.

I walked to the bike's rear and checked the trailer. I rattled the drawbar. It stayed in place, so I drove in. Jazz swam after me.

I remembered to keep the bikes' revs up.

I remembered not to go too fast.

The trailer remained attached.

Jazz shook himself violently on the far bank. His long tongue hung out. He contemplated me.

I opened the paddock's gate, turned the bike off, and inhaled the silence.

A distant tractor revved its engine on a farm across the river.

I rested my hands on my hips and breathed in the scent of the paddocks.

The scent of the cows.

The scent of the grass.

The scent of the countryside.

The flooded river had strewn driftwood over the entire paddock; small branches and entire trees, their roots displayed like incinerated spaghetti. Long grass grew up the sides of each piece.

I filled the trailer with any timber small enough to lift. The afternoon sun burned my arms, and I tugged my Massey Ferguson baseball cap over my eyes.

Inquisitive cows in the neighbouring field congregated next to the fence. They leant across the top wire and inspected my activities.

Good afternoon, ladies. Room service. Won't be long. Sorry to disturb you.

I added small twigs to the pile in the trailer and drove forward. Jazz panted on the tray behind me. A lump of wood dropped off.

If I can reverse the trailer to the edge of the river, I can push the driftwood straight in.

I backed the trailer and it jackknifed.

I drove the trailer in a circle. Another stick fell from the pile.

Each time I reversed, the disobedient Tesco's trolley trailer swung to one side.

I threw my hands up.

This is impossible.

I parked as close as I could to the river and threw the wood down the bank, forming a pile on the grey, pebble riverbed. Sweat ran down my forehead and stung my eyes, as I drove the bike back through the creek and stopped on the far side.

Jazz lapped noisily. I splashed my head, formed a cup with my hands, and swallowed cool, fresh, pure water.

My sleeve made a handy napkin, as I returned to the farmhouse.

"You're burnt," said Fiona. "Did you have sunscreen on? The sun's fierce here. There's a vast hole in the ozone layer above New Zealand."

"The sweat poured off me," I said, as I slurped a cup of tea Linda had produced. "Thank goodness for the creek. I drank a lot of it; this country water tastes so fresh."

Angela burst out laughing.

Linda gaped and stared. "You didn't drink from the creek, did you?"

"What's wrong with drinking out of the creek?" I asked. "It's so clear. It's like an aquarium."

"Well," said Angela. She folded her arms and savoured her forthcoming explanation. "You know how the creek flows through the farm?"

"Yes," I said.

"Before it reaches the crossing where you had your drink, it runs near the milking shed."

"Yes," I said again. I wasn't certain where this conversation was heading.

"What did you help Dad with after milking?"

"I washed the yard with the big hose."

"Yep, what were you hosing away?"

"Cow muck." I said, "loads of it."

"Correct," said Angela, "and where does it end up, once you've washed it out of the yard?"

A dawn of realization peeked above my mental horizon.

"It discharges into the creek?"

"It discharges into the creek. You just drank cow poo, city boy."

Linda grinned and held out a plate. "Another piece of chocolate cake, Simon?"

≈≈≈

Frank squirted the cows' udders with the ochre spray. He stepped out of the concrete channel and opened the gate. Twelve cows walked out, and he clanged it shut. He changed sides and released the other twelve. Phillip flipped the cups onto the new cows.

I loitered at the end of the shed. Frank glanced at his watch.

"Simon," he said, "could you take over the spraying? There's something, erm, important on the radio in a few minutes."

He handed me the bottle.

"As soon as Phillip takes the cups off each cow, give them a spray with this whatsernames. When all twelve on each side finish, you can open the gate."

Phillip grinned at me. "Think you can manage that?"

"I reckon so."

I stood like an Olympic runner on the starting blocks, poised to squirt my first customer.

The cows chewed the cud. I attempted to emulate their circular mouth motion and wondered how it felt to have milk sucked out of you.

Scenicland FM played 'Broken Wings' by Mr. Mister.

"This seems to be a popular song," I said.

Phillip nodded. "I think the local radio station only has about five CDs."

"How do you know when the cows have finished giving milk?" I asked.

"Experience," he said. "And these little sight glasses."

In the middle of each black hose, a small, transparent, egg-shaped section allowed a farmer to observe milk splashing up the tube.

I inspected each glass.

Some cows' milk flowed faster than others.

Phillip removed the milking machine from the first cow to finish.

"Doesn't give much milk, that one," he said.

"Could I have a guess at which one's going to finish next?" I asked.

"All right," said Phillip.

I watched the sight glasses.

Milk splashed through all of them.

"This cow?" I asked.

"Nope," said Phillip. "She milks slowly."

I continued watching.

"This one?"

"Not her," said Phillip. "She gives milk, stops, then starts again."

This seemed to be an inexact science.

"You missed it," said Phillip, as he removed the machine from a different cow.

I squirted the cow's udder with the ochre spray.

Is this all I'm going to be able to do? Squirt a spray bottle?

The cows finished one by one.

"You ready on the gate?" called Phillip.

I hopped up and opened it.

The cows walked out.

Ten cows, eleven cows, twelve cows.

I slammed the gate on cow thirteen.

Phillip flicked the milking cups onto a new set of twelve cows, turned around, and removed the machine from the last cow on the opposite side of the herringbone.

"Other gate?" he called.

I opened the gate on the right-hand side.

One cow, two, three,

Phillip rinsed the metal rails with the small hose.

Nine cows, ten, eleven,

Jazz licked at a puddle of milk. I patted him with my spare hand.

Cow thirteen squeezed past cow number twelve and shoved through the gate.

"Phillip," I shouted. "Help."

10. FROSTY THE SNOWMAN

Phillip sprinted out of the shed. He waved his arms in front of the cow and shouted. He steered her to the yard entrance and let her in with her colleagues.

I rubbed my chin.

"Sorry, Phillip. I stopped to pat the dog and accidentally allowed an extra one through."

"All right, Simon. It's not a major problem. We'll milk her next turn."

Phillip continued applying the milking cups to the udders.

"..you're listening to 93.1 Scenicland FM broadcasting all along the West Coast. It's 4:50 p.m.; we'll have an overnight low of thirteen degrees. News is coming up on the hour, so while you're dreaming of Santa, sit back, and 'Take It Easy' with the Eagles."

I folded my hands in front of me and contemplated my feet.

I'd lost the trailer in the creek, drunk cow poo, and released cows that hadn't been milked.

My aim to impress Fiona's family wasn't exactly going to plan.

I picked up the spray bottle, squirted udders, and opened the gate for the final group of cows. Their tails flicked from side-to-side as they followed their herd along the track.

"I'll lock the cows in," said Phillip. "You all right to finish up here?"

"Of course, Phillip. No problem."

He walked out, and I heard the kick-start of his motorbike.

I grabbed the big, white hose, washed the muck from the yard, and turned the water off.

I stood alone in the shed.

I stepped into the concrete channel and walked between the two rows of dripping milking machines, cleaned and hitched up, ready for the morning's operations.

I stroked the milking cups that attached to the cows' udders.

I inspected the sight glasses and caressed the rubbery, black hoses.

I held my chin high and set my jaw.

I'm going to learn to milk these cows by myself.

I'm going to show Frank and Phillip a pen-pusher can become a farmer.

I slammed the shed gates and walked to the house for dinner.

≈≈≈

Frank furrowed his brow. He set down his knife and fork and gazed out of the window.

"Everything all right, Frank?" I asked. "Anything I can help with?"

"You're enthusiastic, I'll give you that."

"How's the grass?" said Linda.

"I'm not sure about the paddocks over the creek," said Frank. "There's a lot of clover. We need to keep an eye on it."

"What's wrong with clover?" I asked. "Is it poisonous to the cows?"

"The opposite," said Frank. "It's chocolate to them and it's beneficial. They love it and gorge themselves. But it produces gas inside them, and their stomachs swell up. You can see their sides puffed out like balloons. We call that 'bloat'."

"Okay," I said, "so why do we have to keep an eye on it?"

"Because their bloated stomachs push against their hearts," said Linda, "and it can kill them."

"Poor cows," said Fiona. "Imagine if you were left in a field full of chocolate, and you ate a lot, and died."

"But what a way to go," said Angela.

Frank ignored his daughters. He cupped his chin in his palm.

I rubbed the back of my neck.

"Is there anything we can do to stop this bloat happening?" I asked.

"There's only one action to perform," said Frank.

"Stab the cow," said Angela. She formed an evil grin and watched for my reaction.

Linda and Frank nodded.

"Stab it?" I frowned. "You mean kill it?"

"Not kill it, stab it," said Frank. "In the side near the hip bone. It releases the gas."

He leant to one side in his chair and produced a long knife from his pocket.

I was reminded of a scene from *Crocodile Dundee*.

"I always carry this. With a bloated cow you don't have much time."

"Does it hurt the cow?" I asked.

"I'm sure it does," said Frank, "but at least it'll live. And if you ever have to stab a cow, stand back. The smell from the escaping gas is, well…"

"As bad as your farts?" said Angela.

≈≈≈

I woke to the sound of scrunching pebbles, leant on my elbows, and pulled back the curtain. A Baskerville-fog of condensation concealed the view, so I squeaked a circle in it and revealed a sky as blue as a Barclay's Bank foyer.

The early morning excitement of a promised hot summer's day and the sight of the steaming cows bounced me out of bed. I tugged on a T-shirt and shorts while Fiona slept.

"Morning, Simon. Happy Christmas." Linda kissed me on the cheek. She turned around and pulled a bag of potatoes from the pantry.

"Christmas," I said. I pushed up my bottom lip. "I forgot."

Cards with Dickensian scenes hung from string. Fake snow crescents decorated window panes. A small Christmas tree stood in a corner, and bright pinpoints of sunshine reflected from its baubles.

Linda clicked on a radio, and I recognised the closing refrain of 'Santa Claus is Comin' to Town'.

"..a very happy Christmas morning to you, from all of us at 93.1 Scenicland FM. The time is 8:15. While the rest of the South Island suffers through fourteen degrees and a strong South-Westerly, we've a perfect Coast day with a light breeze and a high of 24. Stay tuned, as we play your favourite Christmas hits. We'll be right back with 'Frosty the Snowman' after this message from our sponsors."

I stared out of the window. Frosty would survive thirteen seconds as a solid object if anyone had built him here.

"It doesn't feel like Christmas," I said.

Linda chopped the potatoes into quarters, bent down, and pulled a large baking tray from a cupboard near her legs.

"Are you going to help with milking?" She glanced at the clock. "They'll be nearly finished."

"Do you need anything done here?"

"Yes please, that'd be great." She juggled Russian doll saucepans and searched for more space on the kitchen counter. "We'll have to rearrange the room; there'll be a lot of us for lunch today."

"Who's coming?"

"Phillip, his wife, and their two wee boys, Fiona's nana and pop, and all of us. Gosh, how many's that?"

"I make it eleven."

"See if you can find enough chairs. The boys can sit on stools. Push the tables together and put these cloths over them. I'll better hurry with the food."

"I love Christmas lunch," I said, as I pulled furniture across the carpet. "Especially bread sauce and Brussels sprouts."

"Bread sauce?" said Linda. "Is that something you eat in England?"

"It's a sauce you have with turkey. Or chicken. It takes two minutes to make with a packet and some milk."

"I've never heard of it." She shoved the metal tray in the oven. "I own an old cookbook from England. I'll see if I can find a recipe. And I'm afraid there won't be any Brussels sprouts. They're a winter vegetable."

My lips pressed together.

"Of course. Winter vegetable; summer Christmas."

I pointed at each chair I'd pushed under the two tables and counted in my head. Nine, plus two stools for the children. The tablecloths didn't match, and I searched the room to find something to disguise the line between them.

Scenicland FM progressed from 'Frosty the Snowman' to 'Winter Wonderland'.

I shielded my eyes from the sun streaming in the window and watched the cows trudge to their Christmas day paddock.

This isn't Christmas. There's no darkness, no anticipation.

I heard Phillip start his motorbike, and watched him follow the herd, his two young sons balanced between his knees, miniature replicas of their father, dressed in identical Wellington boots.

A jolly lady carrying a tray of vegetables bumped the kitchen door open.

"Hello, Simon. I'm Adrienne, Phillip's wife. Those are my two terrors on the bike with him."

She bashed the tray down on the table, disrupting my carefully laid cloth.

"Pleased to meet you, Adrienne," I said.

"Back in a minute. I've a few loads to bring in."

She left, and I heard breaking glass followed by an expletive.

"Are you okay?" I poked my head out.

Adrienne barged past and crashed several bags on the floor.

"D'you have a broom, Linda? I dropped a bottle of wine."

≈≈≈

"Where the hell's Nana?" asked Linda, as she removed a pterodactyl-sized turkey from the oven. "She's late."

Frank grinned and poured two glasses of whisky. "Are you having a dig at your mother again?"

He offered me a tumbler. I took it and wondered whether whisky benefited pot plants or killed them.

"She's forgotten what life's like on a farm," said Linda. "You'd have thought after farming for forty years herself she'd remember. If she's not here with her trifle in five minutes, we're starting without her."

"What's the rush?" I asked.

"Afternoon milking's at 3:30. If we don't start Christmas lunch now, we won't finish in time, and nobody can relax."

"You don't sound relaxed at the moment," said Frank. He sipped his Glenmorangie.

"I'm not," said Linda, threatening the air with a carving knife.

"Frank, would you like me to help with milking this afternoon?" I asked.

"I tell you what," said Frank, "how about you and I do the milking, and Phillip can have Christmas afternoon with his kids."

"That'd be nice," said Adrienne. She shoved her boys' stools towards the table.

"D'you think I've enough experience?" I asked.

"I'll attach the milking cups to the cows," said Frank, "and I'll remove them as well. You can perform the spraying and work the gate."

"Make sure you don't let any cows through until they've been milked," said Phillip. He gave me a big wink as he slurped a beer. The froth stuck to his moustache.

I limited myself to two drinks. I didn't want to make any more mistakes.

≈≈≈

3:30.

Milking time.

Even on Christmas day.

Frank set down his whisky, pushed on the arms of his chair, stood up, and put his hands on his hips.

"Right-ho, Simon. Could you drive the whatsernames and fetch the cows? They're in the paddock behind the house."

He pointed at the grey pebble path leading outside Fiona's bedroom window.

"Head up there and you'll find them. Circle the field to make sure you haven't missed any and remember to shut the gate when they're all out. That's the important bit."

Phillip leant back in his chair and poured another beer. He turned to his wife, and grinned.

"It's nice to have the afternoon off," he said. "I'm enjoying having this new farm worker."

Laughter followed this statement, but I smiled to myself.

I'm a farm worker.

≈≈≈

The afternoon sun burned the back of my neck as I drove the four-wheel bike along the gravel path. Jazz panted behind me. He licked my ear, and I squirmed.

I mentally rehearsed my responsibilities.

One—fetch the cows. Two—check there are none left in the paddock. Three—shut the gate. Four—squirt the udders. Five—release twelve each side.

Two hundred cows mustered at the field entrance. They mooed simultaneously, like an unruly meeting before the chairperson brings it to order. I opened the gate and held it politely.

"Off you go, girls," I said. "Enjoy."

The last cows walked out, and I bumped the bike into the field. Jazz ran alongside and barked.

We circumnavigated the perimeter. I checked down the banks of the creek, searching for any stragglers.

No cows.

I checked in the trees at the edge.

No cows.

I checked in the clump of bushes in the centre of the paddock.

No cows.

Jazz and I headed out of the field.

I remembered to close the gate.

Frank had finished the first set of 24. I watched him remove the milking machine from the udders slowly and deliberately. He'd been doing this all his life.

I walked between the two rows of cows, squirting their teats with the ochre anti-mastitis liquid. Frank constantly rinsed everything with his little hose: the milking machine, his hands, the rails of the shed. 205 cows generated a lot of muck.

"Ready to open the thingamy, Simon?" He pointed at the gate.

I hopped out of the central concrete channel and released the cows on one side. Twelve walked through. Number thirteen tried to escape early. I shouted and waved my arms. The cow paused, and I slammed the gate.

Did you see, Frank? I didn't let the cow through.

Frank smiled and turned away.

I opened the gate on the other side, counted twelve cows and closed it.

Frank had his back turned.

He fitted the milking machine to the next udders.

He didn't watch me work the gate.

I took a deep breath and enjoyed the moment.

"Well done," said Frank. "You've mastered that component of the operation."

"Could I try taking the milking cups off now? I mean, could you tell me when the cow's finished giving milk, and I'll remove them?"

"Of course," said Frank. "Be careful not to let any cups drop on the ground. They don't stop pulsing when you remove them, and we don't want any cow muck sucked into the milk vat."

I watched the cows stand patiently while the milking machine pumped.

I studied the little sight glasses. Milk pulsed through all of them.

"They give a lot of milk, don't they?"

"This time of year, their yield's high. As we progress further into Autumn they slow down, and we dry them off for winter."

I waited.

"This one's ready," said Frank.

I grasped the first milking cup and pulled it off the teat. It dangled close to the ground.

"Careful," said Frank.

He grabbed the cup and turned it upwards.

I removed the second cup. I held it off the floor.

I removed the third cup.

I needed six hands and thirty fingers to hold all the bits of the machine and take it off the udders.

I had no idea how Frank and Phillip did it so quickly.

Frank still clutched the first cup.

I removed the fourth, and with a flourish worthy of a Shakespearian actor, I pulled the whole machine away from the cow.

Frank grinned.

"Well done, Simon. We'll attempt another one in a minute."

"I think I'll watch you do some more," I said. "I don't feel very confident at that part yet."

I picked up the ochre liquid.

≈≈≈

The last cows ambled to their new pasture.

Frank turned the milking machine off.

"..we hope you've enjoyed your sunny Christmas afternoon. This is 93.1 Scenicland FM broadcasting all along the West Coast. The time's 5:55, and we'll head to Patricia for news and weather, after these messages."

Frank clicked the radio off, and I heard the trickle of water as he rinsed the milking equipment with the little hose.

"Would you like me to wash the yard and lock the cows in?" I said. "You could go and enjoy Christmas day with your family."

"Are you sure? It's your Christmas too."

"I'm enjoying myself here," I said.

"All right," said Frank, "but don't feel anything's compulsory."

I picked up the big hose and sluiced the muck from the yard.

Frank put his hands on his hips and watched me. He smiled, nodded, and departed.

The lava of cow muck spread towards the grate and disappeared through the hole in the side of the shed. I turned off the hose.

Jazz stood next to the four-wheel bike, with his head on one side, and his tongue hanging out.

I turned the bike's key, and he hopped on the back.

We followed a fresh trail of cow droppings along the track, steaming in the evening sun like a series of brandied Christmas puddings.

I drove the bike through the creek, stopped it at the entrance to the cows' field, and stepped off.

The herd stood scattered across the paddock with their heads down, eating their Christmas dinner.

I narrowed my eyebrows and peered.

Something wasn't right.

One cow looked unbalanced.

I studied another cow near her to compare.

The second cow seemed normal.

I returned my gaze to the first cow and rubbed the back of my neck.

Is this bloat? I don't want to make a fuss about nothing.

The lopsided cow raised her head at me and paused, mid-munch.

She appeared to be happy and resumed cud-chewing. Her jaw rotated like a Kenwood mixer on cake setting.

I walked away from her, turned around, and latched the gate.

The cow and I met eyes.

As if an invisible giant had shoved her sideways, she toppled over.

Dead.

11. TOM CRUISE

Shit.

Help.

The cows are dying.

Fetch someone, quick.

I hopped on the four-wheel bike and sped back along the track.

Jazz ran after me. I heard his barks fade.

A bow wave of water rose in front of me as I ploughed through the creek.

Slow down. Don't drown the bike.

I bounced along the grey pebble track, through the potholes, past Shazam, to the farmhouse. The fence posts blurred. I wasn't sure of the bike's top speed, but I couldn't pull the throttle any harder.

Fiona's family sat in the garden enjoying the Christmas evening sun. They drank beer and wine, nibbled left-overs, laughed, and chatted.

They looked up as I skidded to a stop.

"Bloat knife!" I shouted. "Need the bloat knife."

Frank was 63 years old.

He had a Glenmorangie in one hand.

He had a spoon of trifle in the other.

I'd never seen a senior citizen move so fast.

He jumped out of his chair and pulled his knife from his pocket.

His glass and spoon fell on the lawn.

He mounted the bike next to me, and we powered along the track.

I stood up on the pedals and sat down again.

How many cows will have survived? Will they all be dead?

We encountered Jazz, who barked, turned around, and sprinted after us, back towards the cows.

Into the creek.

Through the creek.

Out of the creek.

We arrived at the gate.

Frank jumped off the bike.

He rolled between the strands of the electric fence like a commando on a training exercise.

He pushed himself to his feet, lifted his hand to his eyes, and surveyed the herd.

The cows raised their heads in mild surprise at being visited twice in one evening. Everything about the scene appeared normal, except for the dead cow who lay where she'd dropped.

I wonder whether cows feel sad when one of their herd passes away.

I climbed over the gate and stood with Frank.

"Are the other cows all right?" I asked.

"One or two look a bit blown up."

Phillip arrived on his motorbike.

He gritted his teeth and smacked his fist into his palm.

"Bloody hell," he said. "She was a good milker."

Frank shook his head at the ground. "We'll have to drench them. Christmas day, of all days."

"Drench them?" I asked. "Wash them down?"

"Feed them medicine," said Frank. "It counteracts the effects of the clover and stops them becoming bloated."

"I'll meet you back at the shed," said Phillip. He roared off, and a plume of dust obscured his bike.

Frank strode to the rear of the herd and called the dog, "Here, Jazz. Here, Jazz."

Jazz barked at the cows.

This perturbed them. They weren't accustomed to relocating in the middle of dinner. Particularly Christmas dinner.

Frank shouted and waved his arms.

I revved the bike's engine.

Jazz barked again.

The cows traipsed out of the gate. Frank walked with them, and I followed the stragglers.

≈≈≈

"They're creatures of habit," said Phillip, as he shut the yard gate behind 204 cows. "They know they shouldn't be in the shed now. Plus, drenching's not a pleasant experience for them."

The cows lined up, twelve on either side of the concrete trench, as if they were re-enacting the afternoon's milking.

"..thank you for sharing your Christmas evening with us. This is 93.1 Scenicland FM, broadcasting all along the wonderful West Coast. We're in for some fine, settled weather over the next week, so enjoy your Christmas holidays and don't touch that dial, it's the 'Jingle Bell Rock'."

I tilted my head to one side and pursed my lips.

"The radio seems too loud. It's odd, being in here without the sound of the milking machine."

I watched Frank's actions.

"We drench them with this bloat oil," he said. He showed me a long, pointy, metal instrument which resembled an exhibit in a Victorian medical museum. A hose led from the bloat drenching tool into a drum of liquid.

Frank grabbed the first cow's head, stuck the pointy contraption down her throat, and pulled a trigger.

Her alarmed, wide eyes indicated she didn't enjoy this ordeal.

The squirting operation lasted a few seconds.

The cow licked her lips, and Frank treated the next one.

On the other side of the walkway, Phillip duplicated the process.

Two hundred and four cows all taking their medicine.

One cow it was too late for.

I studied the ground with my hands in my pockets.

Frank put his hand on my shoulder.

"It's all right, Simon. You did the right thing, coming to fetch me. Death's a regular occurrence on a farm. Townies who purchase their meat and milk from the supermarket are shielded from these circumstances."

I looked up.

Did Frank just exclude me from the category of 'townies'?

He paused.

"D'you want to help me bury the cow?" he asked.

"How do we do that? It must take a long time to dig the hole."
"Not when you own a tractor."

≈≈≈

Frank opened tall, metal double doors and pointed at a red tractor with a scoop on the front.

He slapped the side twice to illustrate where I should sit. I jumped up and balanced on the left mud guard.

We drove towards the field that I would forever know as 'dead cow paddock'.

Along the track.

Past Shazam.

Through the creek, which barely rinsed the tractor's tyres.

The cow still lay where she'd fallen. This shouldn't have surprised me, but I wasn't prepared for the sight of her body by itself in the paddock. Cows were supposed to be grouped in a herd.

Frank pulled heavy chains out of the tractor's bucket.

He wrapped them around the cow's legs.

I wondered how many times he'd been a bovine funeral director.

He stepped up on the tractor and pulled a lever.

The tractor's bucket lifted, and the chains suspended the cow upside down in the air, a position she would never have assumed during her living years.

Her tongue hung out.

My eyes watered, and the corners of my mouth turned down.

Frank lurched the tractor through potholes towards the river.

The cow swung from the chains, as if she played on an undignified, morbid trapeze.

Frank stopped the tractor on the riverbed.

He lowered the dead cow.

She lay on the pebbles with her tongue still hanging out.

I stepped off the tractor and stood back.

Frank unclipped the chains, pointed the scoop into the pebbles, and dug.

He formed a mound of stones.

I wondered how many cows he'd buried out here. Would future archaeologists excavate the river and conclude twentieth century New Zealanders engaged in ritual bovine massacre?

Frank kept his mouth in a straight line, and his white tufts of hair blew in the breeze.

He assessed he'd dug a large enough grave and reattached the chains.

He stepped back on the tractor.

I touched the cow's flank.

She still felt warm.

Warm and furry.

She didn't feel dead.

Frank lifted her again.

He placed her in the hole.

He pushed the pebbles with the tractor's scoop, until he'd buried every part of black-and-white.

Her ear was the last bit to disappear.

Linda placed a ham sandwich in front of me.

"Fiona's nana phoned. She wonders if you could call around and help her hang their front door? Pop took it off for her to paint, but it's too heavy for them to lift back on again. Honestly, I don't know why they attempt these jobs at their age."

"I'd be happy to. Does she need me immediately?"

"I think so. Take my car. She said there'd be trifle."

"I'm on my way."

I stuffed the sandwich in, pulled my shoes on, and headed into town.

Farm vehicles approached. I offered the West Coast index-finger greeting to each one, and I grinned and nodded as they returned the signal.

They think I'm a local.

≈≈≈

I shaded my eyes with my hand and gazed across the whole of Hokitika from Fiona's grandparents' hillside home, taking in the endless sea, the grid of detached wooden houses, and, in front of the mountains, the runway of the local airport.

I could hardly see Nana's tiny frame above the kitchen counters. Her mop of white, curly hair bobbed between the fridge and the sink.

She placed a bowl in front of me and squelched out a portion of trifle. It spilt over the edge.

"Is that enough, Simon? You working men need feeding up."

The jelly wobbled on my spoon, and I shoved it in my mouth before it had a chance to fall onto the dining-room table.

The buzz of a small plane distracted me. I watched it fly outside Nana's window, as if I could reach up and snatch it from the sky.

"Are those planes allowed to take off so close to the commercial airport?" I asked.

Pop lowered his newspaper, removed his spectacles, and laughed. "They are taking off from the commercial airport. The Christchurch flight comes in three times a day. It's nothing like your London terminals. After you've eaten your trifle, why don't you drive past and have a look?"

"Okay, it sounds interesting. I've a few spare hours before afternoon milking."

≈≈≈

I changed gear and climbed the hill to the airport. Thick native bush tumbled down to the road, and to my right the mountain tops contoured against a heat-hazy sky. This was hardly the M4 motorway to Heathrow.

The terminal car park contained five cars. I was about to walk to a low fence and investigate the runway, when I noticed a sandwich board positioned by a hangar.

'Ever wanted to be a pilot? Take a trial flight today. Thirty minutes for forty dollars.'

I put my hand in my pocket, found two twenty-dollar notes, and walked through the hangar onto the asphalt.

A man in a checked shirt, shorts and boots leant against a worryingly minuscule propeller aircraft.

"Can I help you?" he said.

"Is this where I can try out to be a pilot?"

He pushed out his bottom lip and put his palm on his chin.

"Be a pilot?"

"Yes," I said, "the board outside advertised a thirty-minute trial flight for forty dollars."

"Mmm, okay. When did you want to go?"

"Now."

"Now? Right now?"

"If possible. I have just over an hour before I need to be elsewhere."

He rotated his wrist, inspected his watch, and scratched the back of his head. He gazed around.

There didn't seem to be a queue of other customers, or indeed anything happening at all. I wondered if my visit was delaying his lunch break.

"Okay, why not?" he said. He pointed at his chest. "I'm Doug."

Black oil stains patterned his fingers.

"Pleased to meet you, Doug. I'm Simon."

"Have you flown a plane before, Simon?"

"Nope. I've never sat further forward than economy class."

I offered him my money.

"Are you on holiday here?" he asked.

"I live on a farm in the valley. I go out with Fiona, Frank and Linda's daughter."

"Oh. You're that Simon."

I wasn't clear on whether being 'that Simon' was a good thing or not.

"All right," said Doug. "Here's what we'll do. I'll explain the plane's features and controls, then we'll fly out to the valley, and we'll try to spot Frank and Linda's farm from the air."

"Gosh," I said. "Yes please."

He slurped from a mug of tea and planted it on the ground.

"The name of this model of plane is a Piper Tomahawk. Before we fly, we run through a three-part checklist. Electrical, mechanical, and chemical. Listen carefully, and I'll explain it."

He strode around the plane. I followed.

"We need to confirm the flap actuators are connected, but mobile."

"Right. The flap actuators."

"Check the bolts connecting the flap to the wing. Confirm the aileron is secured to the wing. Check the screws are solid, and the pins are at ninety-degree angles."

I scratched my head.

"Have a pull on the aileron. You should see the yoke move."

"What's the yoke?"

"The yoke is the plane's steering wheel. Make sure the wing tip's anchored by giving it a good shake."

Doug shook the wing. The entire plane wobbled alarmingly, like a spoonful of Nana's trifle.

"Check the stall warning tab on the wing. Ensure the horizontal tail stabilizer is free, and your trim tabs move in the correct direction. Check that the rudder moves."

Do I have to remember all this?

Doug led me to the front of the plane.

"Check your air inlets and exhaust for any birds' nests or other rubbish. Check the propeller blades. Make sure they're firmly fixed with no dents. Dip the petrol tank. Ensure it agrees with the fuel gauge."

He lifted a hatch on one side of the engine.

"Open both sides of the engine cowling. Check your oil, spark plugs, and your wires connected to your magneto, including the hot wire that attaches to the battery. Check your brake fluid level. Check all wires are fixed, and connected to the fuel pump."

I stared at the plane's innards.

"D'you understand everything so far?" said Doug.

"Erm, some of it I think. But you mentioned we should open both sides of the engine cowling. You only opened one."

Doug clenched his teeth and turned his head slowly towards me.

"Very good. I was just confirming you were listening."

He unfastened the other side, peeked inside, and shut it again.

"All right, that's the exterior checks complete. Climb up the wing and hop in."

I imagined the interior would resemble a 1980s rock star's jet with tiger-coloured seats and shag-pile carpet.

I stepped up and opened the door.

A pair of red vinyl seats, devoid of headrests, perched in front of an array of dials in a Formica dashboard, with twin steering wheels poking out of them.

Not steering wheels, Simon. They're called yokes.

I noticed a tear in my seat fabric and took care not to increase it. My head swivelled as I stared out of the all-round windows.

Doug continued my education.

"Turn on all the master switches and check the fuel gauges. Listen for the fuel pump running."

He cupped his hand to his ear and tilted his head.

"Check all the lights work."

He flicked switches up and down. I'd long since abandoned any hope of keeping up with his instructions.

Doug handed me a set of headphones with a microphone on a stalk.

"Put these on your ears," he said. "We can talk to each other through the headset. If you push this button here, we can communicate with Control."

Doug's tinny voice echoed from the end of a very long tunnel.

"This is a training plane," he said. "It features dual instruments and controls, so either of us can fly it. I'll do most of the flying, and I'll tell you when it's time to take over."

Take over.

Me.

Flying an actual plane.

"The key thing with flying," said Doug, "is to touch as little as possible. Don't make any sudden changes to the controls. Slow and gentle. Are you ready?"

My heartbeat increased, and an image of Tom Cruise in a green uniform entered my mind.

I smiled.

Simon. You're going to Top Gun.

"Let's do it." I said.

Doug turned a knob labelled *fuel*, pushed a lever, and started the engine with a key, like a car ignition.

He eased the throttle forward.

"We'll taxi to the runway," said Doug, "and we'll request permission to take off."

I watched the propeller rotate, and the plane progressed.

As we halted at a white line, I heard a voice in my headphones that I wasn't expecting.

12. PAMELA ANDERSON

It wasn't Doug's voice speaking in the headphones.

"Hokitika Control, Hokitika Control. This is Alpha November Zulu eight-eight-three-six. Request permission to land."

"Alpha November Zulu eight-eight-three-six, Hokitika Control. Good afternoon to you. Cleared to land runway two-one to the west."

"Thank you, Hokitika Control. Alpha November Zulu eight-eight-three-six confirming landing runway two-one to the west."

"That's the lunchtime flight from Christchurch," said Doug. "We'll hold and wait for him."

"Are we taking off on the same runway?" I asked.

"There's only one in use," said Doug.

This is crazy.

I'm about to fly a plane.

From the same runway as Air New Zealand.

"If you look towards the mountains," said Doug, "you'll be able to see the Metroliner on approach."

"Metroliner?"

"The Air New Zealand plane. The one you heard talking to Control."

I peered at the mountains and turned my head left and right.

"How far away is he?" I asked.

"He'll have requested permission to land once he cleared the Alps. Keep watching. Look higher. Here he is."

Doug pointed.

I fixed my eyes on a hornet-sized dot descending in the distance.

I blinked.

It looked odd to watch it fly below the peaks of the mountains. Planes should fly in the sky.

The hornet grew bigger, as we held our position.

The Metroliner performed dramatic wobbles before it landed, as if the pilot had elected to offer the passengers some last-minute excitement for the price of their ticket.

"Bang on time," said Doug, looking at his watch. "1:55 p.m."

As the engine noise of the twin-propeller, pointy-nosed Air New Zealand plane decreased, it semi-circled at the end of the runway, and stopped in front of the terminal. Through its windscreen, I observed two pilots in white uniforms adjust controls.

"Ready for take-off?" said Doug.

I gripped my hands together and swallowed a croquet-ball sized lump in my throat.

"I'm ready."

I heard his voice in the headphones.

"Hokitika Control, Hokitika Control. This is Echo Sierra Golf. Request permission to take off."

"Echo Sierra Golf, Hokitika Control. Good afternoon to you. Cleared to take-off runway two-one to the west."

"Thank you, Hokitika Control. Echo Sierra Golf confirming taking off runway two-one to the west."

"Simon," said Doug. "Don't touch any controls until I tell you."

"Of course. I'm not going to breathe until you tell me."

The propeller rotated as the Piper Tomahawk taxied.

I felt the vibration increase and the seat pushed in my back, as we accelerated and took off.

Nana's house disappeared behind Doug's right shoulder.

The dials in front of me spun.

"We need to climb at seventy knots," said Doug.

He turned the yoke, and my window pointed towards the ground. I held the door handle, in case it opened, and I plummeted to my death.

"We're at four thousand feet," said Doug, as the plane levelled. "Want to take over?"

"Erm, okay."

"Keep her flying straight. I'll tell you when to turn."

Below me, the beach extended in a satin ribbon of yellow-brown, with a parallel white stripe stitching it to the endless blue sea.

We flew across the ocean.

Away from the land.

Four thousand feet of vacuous air underneath me, carpeted by deep, freezing Tasman Sea.

I fought the urge to turn the wheel and head back to Hokitika and safety.

We won't make it to Australia, Doug. It's time to turn around.

Doug stared ahead. His hands lay in his lap.

Are we still supposed to be flying out to sea? I can't keep quiet any longer.

"Erm, when do we turn, Doug?"

"Whenever you like. Let's circle her to the left, so we're parallel to the coast."

I grinned as the Piper Tomahawk responded to my hand movements.

Careful, Simon. No acrobatics.

The coastline of New Zealand turned to meet me.

The plane flew parallel to the beach.

I sat up straight and gripped the yoke.

I'm Tom Cruise.

I've gone to Top Gun.

"D'you see Mount Camelback?" asked Doug.

Viewed from ground level, the hill protruded, as if a giant, green Pamela Anderson lay on her back.

"Got it," I said.

"Turn us towards it."

Doug's hands still lay in his lap.

I turned, and we aimed for Camelback.

"How are you feeling?" asked Doug. "Getting the hang of it?"

"Great, thanks. Enjoying myself."

My grip on the steering wheel loosened.

"Let's descend and look at the farm," said Doug.

"Okay. How do we do that?"

"I'll help you. We ease the throttle back, and let the nose drop, to control the rate of descent."

Doug pulled the throttle, and we descended.

I identified Frank and Linda's farmhouse.

I hope Fiona's outside to watch me flying a plane. This would impress her so much.

"Where's the main herd today?" asked Doug.

"There." I pointed at a group of black-and-white dots.

"Turn her left in a wide circle."

Cows ran across a field below me.

I'm a wildlife photographer on African safari. My pictures of migrating wildebeest will make a stunning accompaniment to my article for National Geographic. All I need to find is some lions and an elephant, and my story will be complete.

"Straighten up," said Doug, "and we'll take her back to the airport."

The farm disappeared as I completed the turn.

Doug pushed the throttle forward, and I watched a dial return to four thousand feet.

I heard his voice in the headphones.

"Hokitika Control, Hokitika Control. Echo Sierra Golf. Request permission to land.

"Echo Sierra Golf, Hokitika Control. Cleared to land runway two-one to the west."

"Thank you, Hokitika Control. Echo Sierra Golf, confirming landing runway two-one to the west."

"It's best if I land her," said Doug.

"Definitely. I've no desire to be the opening item on Scenicland FM's news."

I let go of the yoke, and Doug controlled our descent.

He taxied and parked the Piper Tomahawk where our Top Gun adventure had started.

I took off my headphones, and my ears rang with the silence.

"Did you enjoy that?" asked Doug. He grinned at me.

"Fantastic, thanks so much. The best forty dollars I've spent."

"If you ever apply for your pilot's licence, those thirty minutes will contribute towards your hours."

"Thanks, Doug. I've got to run. I can't be late for milking."

≈≈≈

I whistled as I drove to the farm and turned at the junction near Camelback mountain.

I opened the kitchen door. Fiona, Frank and Angela sat at the dining-room table. Linda arranged cakes on a plate.

I hummed and pulled my shoes off.

"What are you looking so happy about?" asked Fiona.

I closed the door and sat in a chair.

"You'll never guess what I did today."

You'll be so proud when you discover you're dating Tom Cruise.

"Go on, tell us," said Fiona.

"So, after I'd finished helping at Nana's, I drove to.."

The kitchen door flung open.

Phillip entered, sat on a chair, and thumped the table.

"Bloody hell," he said. "I've just about had enough of this."

13. HIPPY VEGETARIAN

"What's wrong with you, Phillip?" said Linda.

"Some bloody idiot in a little plane flew low over the farm and spooked the cows. I wish I'd grabbed the registration number. Shazam broke out of his paddock and fought with the other bulls. It took me ages to separate them. And now I'll have to fix his fence."

"That's no good," said Linda. She plunked a mug of tea in front of him.

He picked it up and slurped it.

I put my hands on my forehead and studied the pattern on the tablecloth.

"Bloody trainee pilots," said Phillip. He clenched his teeth and sucked in a breath. "They should find somewhere else to perform their acrobatics."

"You were saying you went somewhere, Simon?" said Fiona.

I glanced up.

"Erm, I took a lovely stroll along the beach. Lots of driftwood. These are yummy cakes, Linda. Did you make them today?"

≈≈≈

The milking machine hummed as I arrived at the shed. Phillip whistled, accompanying Scenicland FM's limited early morning repertoire.

I stood with my hands in my pockets and watched him work.

"Would you like to learn how to take the cups off the cows?" asked Phillip.

"Erm, Frank let me try one at Christmas, but he had to help me. I need to be an octopus to hold all four cups at once."

Phillip laughed. "Watch me. I'll show you."

He pointed to one of the egg-shaped sight-glasses embedded in a black rubber hose. "This one's finished. See, there's a dribble coming through. Compare her with the next cow. She's still milking."

I inspected the two sight glasses.

Phillip removed the cups and held them upwards, so they didn't suck cow manure into the milk vat.

"Got that, Simon?"

"Could you show me again, please? Slower."

Phillip grinned. "Right-oh. This one's ready."

I studied the master at work. Phillip demonstrated his precise technique. He flicked the milking cups up and held them out of the way. I mimed with my empty hands, copying his movements.

"You have a try," he said. "Which cow's next? I'll give you a clue; there are three ready."

"This one?" I pointed.

"Correct," said Phillip.

I hesitated.

"You'd better hurry," said Phillip. "There are seven more after her." He rinsed the set of cups he'd removed.

I pulled the first cup off the teat and tried to repeat the mime. I pulled the second one and held the first and second. The third lay above them in my upturned palm.

I need big farmers' hands.

I pulled the fourth, stepped back before any cups fell on the ground, hung the cups on the hook, and studied Phillip's face for approval.

He grinned. "Next one, Simon. We'll be here all day at this rate."

One cow still gave milk. I pulled the other cups off one by one and hung them up. I returned to the slow cow, tugged off the last cups, and completed the twelve.

"Well done," said Phillip. "You'll be milking by yourself soon."

My chest swelled, and I grinned and raised my eyebrows.

"You'd better give them a spray. There's the other side to do next."

I grabbed the ochre liquid, squirted the udders, and began to remove the cups from the animals on the other side.

This'll impress Frank so much when I tell him.

≈≈≈

"Frank, guess what I can do?"

"Go on," said Frank's voice from behind yesterday's paper. "What can you do?"

I stood with my hands tucked into my armpits.

"I can take the cups off the cows without dropping them. I can even tell which cow's ready to finish."

Frank lowered the paper. "Isn't that wonderful? It still amazes me that a city boy wants to get his hands dirty."

"Leave him alone," said Linda. "It's all new and exciting to him."

Frank replaced his glasses, spread the newspaper over the table, and ran his finger down a list of horse races.

"What's for dinner tonight?" I asked.

"Steak and vegetables," said Linda.

I recalled the dead cow's warm body.

"Erm, I don't feel like steak tonight. Could I maybe have some cheese with the vegetables?"

"Not like you, Simon. All right, I'll take one less piece of meat out of the fridge."

"Would you be interested in learning some more farming?" asked Frank.

"Anything," I said. "Tell me what needs doing."

"It's a two-person job. You'll need someone to help."

"Fiona?" I asked, "are you busy today?"

Fiona looked at me as if I'd proposed running naked down Hokitika High Street.

"I don't want to do anything with cows," she said. "You can milk them all you want, but they scare the willies out of me."

Linda laughed. "You're more of a townie than your boyfriend."

"This doesn't involve cows," said Frank. "Have you ever driven a tractor, Simon?"

"I've only ridden on the side with you. Is it different to driving a car?"

"It's bigger, for starters. And slower. But the gears and the pedals operate similarly. If I show you how to drive one, could you take it into the paddocks and spray weed killer on the gorse? Fiona can walk behind and hold the spray gun. You'll both need to wear masks; you don't want to inhale the chemicals."

"Erm, okay, I'll have a try."

I had a vision of a red tractor lying on its side in the creek.

"Would you help me, Fiona?"

"There won't be any cows in those paddocks, will there?" she asked. "Any that have escaped from other fields?"

"Definitely not," said Frank. "We don't spray near the cattle. I'll show you which gorse needs treatment."

"All right," said Fiona. "I suppose I should do my bit."

≈≈≈

Frank patted the bonnet of a tractor I hadn't seen before.

"This is my Massey Ferguson 55, said Frank. "It's pretty old, but it still runs. When I bought her, all my neighbours asked me why I needed such a big tractor. Today I reckon it's the smallest in the valley. We call it 'the little tractor'."

The little tractor. I'm sure that's the title of an Enid Blyton children's story.

"Hop up, and I'll explain how she works."

Despite its diminutive name, the tractor's rear wheels reached my shoulders.

"You'd better wear something on your head," said Fiona. "You don't want to be burnt again."

She discovered an old floppy hat of Frank's in the corner of the shed.

I sat in the driver's seat and studied the controls. All the labels had worn off decades ago.

My feet reached two pedals. I placed my hands on a complicated signal-box of levers connected to black hoses, shrugged, and raised my eyebrows.

"The left pedal's the clutch," said Frank, "and the right pedal's the brake."

"Okay," I said. "But where's the accelerator?"

"The throttle," said Frank, "is this stick thingamy here."

He pointed at a stalk protruding from under the steering wheel.

"Oh. I thought that controlled the windscreen wipers."

Frank laughed. "Why would you need windscreen wipers? There's no windscreen."

Oh yes. Stupid city boy.

Frank pointed between my feet. "These are the gear levers."

"Why are there two of them?"

"The left one's a gearstick, the same as a car. The other's used to select high or low range. Keep it in high range while driving on the tracks, and low range once you enter the paddocks. Don't concern yourself with these other levers. You won't need them today."

Frank reached up, turned a key, and my entire body vibrated as the engine rumbled. Smoke puffed from the vertical exhaust which wobbled alarmingly.

Jazz barked and ran around the tractor.

Frank shouted. "Ready? Press down on the whatsernames." He pointed.

I pushed the left-hand pedal. I found I needed to stand up to depress it the whole way.

"Move the throttle lever up."

Throttle lever? Oh yes, windscreen wipers.

I nudged the throttle lever. The engine noise increased, and a plume of smoke rose.

"Let the clutch in," said Frank.

I lifted my left foot. The tractor crept forward.

"Don't ride the clutch," said Frank. "Lift your foot all the way."

The tractor moved faster. I hesitated and pushed my foot down again.

The tractor stopped rolling.

"Excellent," shouted Frank. "You've mastered that. Start with the paddocks behind the house."

Is that it? Have I passed my agricultural driving test?

≈≈≈

Fiona opened a gate, and the tractor bumped gently into a field.

"Don't drive too near the edge," said Fiona. "Dad won't thank you if you roll her over."

Fiona patrolled behind the tractor. She brandished her wand and squirted poison at the gorse. I'd never seen her dressed in farming clothes and Wellington boots. I smiled and felt a warm sensation inside; the style suited her.

We jolted across the field, following the creek. Blue-and-black birds with red beaks fled from small clumps of vegetation as we approached.

Fiona pulled her face mask tight and covered the gorse with a fine mist of weed killer. She seemed happy with her task.

I wonder if one day we could run a farm together? Milking the cows, living the outdoor country life, no more offices, no more commuting, no more stress.

Fiona tugged her mask away from her mouth. "How much more is there to do? I bloody hate this job."

≈≈≈

We circumnavigated the field and returned to the gate.

Fiona threw down the spray wand and stumped away to have a shower. I engaged the clutch, pushed the throttle lever, and bumped along the track.

Frank held a big spanner in his right hand. He looked up when he heard my tractor approach.

"How d'you get on?" he asked.

"Great, I loved it. D'you have any other tractor jobs?"

"There's always something to keep you occupied on a farm. How about you take the big tractor and mow the driveway verge? If you're comfortable with that you could cut some paddocks. After that, the superphosphate needs distributing. You'll need two tractors for that job, the loader tractor to fill the phosphate cart and the big tractor to tow it around the paddocks. Oh, and you could pull the silage wagon out. We'll be cutting winter feed soon."

He paused, removed his tin hat, and scratched his head.

"That is," he said, "only if you want to."

"Erm, I'll start with the mowing if that's okay. You'd better show me how the big tractor works."

"All right. We'll have lunch first."

≈≈≈

Frank and I sat at the dining table. Fiona walked in, rubbing a towel through her hair.

"Don't ever ask me to do any more spraying. I've shampooed three times to remove the smell."

Linda laughed. "Fiona's never been interested in farming. You're happier in a city, aren't you?"

Fiona ignored her.

"What's for lunch, Linda?" I asked. "The outdoor air makes me hungry."

"Hamburgers."

The thought of eating cow once in a day, let alone twice, didn't fill me with joy.

"I'll make a salad sandwich, thanks."

Linda pursed her lips and peered at me.

"You're not turning into one of those hippy vegetarians, I hope?"

"Not at all. I'll be back to normal soon. I'm not used to eating this much beef."

≈≈≈

Frank slid a shed door open and revealed a larger, newer tractor with a black cab to shelter the driver.

"How many tractors d'you own?" I asked.

"Three. There's the little tractor you used for spraying."

"The Massey Ferguson 55?"

Frank smiled. "That's the one. Next, the tractor we used to bury the cow with the front-end-loader."

"Which model's that?"

"It's a 174—4. The 'four' at the end denotes the four-wheel-drive version. There's a 172—2 available as well."

Frank patted the bonnet of the big tractor.

"This cab tractor's a 275. It's fairly new; I've owned it a few years. The controls are similar. You'll manage fine."

I scaled two metal rungs and perched in the driver's seat. Frank watched.

I turned a key, and the engine echoed inside the steel shed.

"Drive her out," said Frank. He slammed the cab door.

The tractor crept out of the shed, and the engine sound changed in the open air.

Frank opened the door.

"See the mower?" he shouted.

I turned around and inspected the rear attachment.

"Keep it lifted. When you're ready to cut the grass, push this thingy to drop the mower and pull this one to engage the PTO."

"PTO? Please Turn Over?"

"Power Take Off," said Frank. "It starts the blades rotating. Off you go."

I drove the tractor across the farmyard towards the drive and stopped on the grass verge. Linda, Fiona, and Angela watched me from the dining-room window. They pointed and grinned.

That's all I need. An audience.

My seat dipped as the mower dropped behind me.

The engine tone changed. Grass clippings sprinkled from the rear. The tractor crept forward in response to my push on the throttle.

I steered around a small rock, reached the end of the verge, swung the tractor around in the road, and re-entered the drive.

My audience left the comfort of the dining room and waited on the track. Angela still wore her pyjamas.

I halted the tractor in the middle of the driveway, turned off the engine and opened the door.

"Look at you go, city boy," said Angela.

"Oh, it's easy," I said. "Similar to driving a car."

"You're never going to want to return to London, are you?" said Linda.

Frank walked up to me. "Well done, you've picked up tractor driving."

"Yep, I didn't find it too hard. What needs doing next?"

"I think, before you undertake anything, you should park her somewhere else."

He pointed behind me, and I followed his finger. At the end of the drive, I watched the Westland Dairy milk tanker enter the farm and storm towards us.

≈≈≈

"Have you been mowing again?" asked Fiona, a few days later.

I washed my hands and wiped them on a towel.

"Yep, I cut a big paddock today. I love driving the tractors. D'you want to come for a ride with me this afternoon?"

"No thanks," said Fiona. "I used to sit in the cab with Dad when I was a little girl. It's so boring."

"I saw the postman," I said. "He gave me the mail."

I extracted three envelopes from my pocket.

"Two for Frank and one for you."

She slit the envelope with a kitchen knife, furrowed her brow, and pursed her lips to one side.

I leant towards her.

"Fiona, what's wrong? What's in the letter?"

14. ROLF HARRIS

Fiona showed me the contents of the envelope.

"There's less than a thousand dollars in our bank account. We'll need to find work, or we'll be broke."

I brewed a mug of tea and sat beside her.

"I haven't seen any jobs advertised in Hokitika, have you? Not work we'd be able to do. They're recruiting car mechanics or milk factory technicians."

"We'll have to travel to Christchurch for city jobs. We could stay with my Auntie Debbie, Mum's sister. She has a spare room."

I avoided her gaze.

"I don't want to leave. I'm getting the hang of farming. I think Frank and Phillip appreciate my efforts."

"It's great being on this permanent holiday," said Fiona, "but we can't live off my parents' charity forever."

"We could apply for jobs from here and head to Christchurch if they sound promising. That way we could stay longer on the farm."

"All right. Let's look in the newspaper classifieds after lunch."

≈≈≈

Fiona cleared the plates and spread the newspaper across the dining room table. She grabbed a pen and sat down. I pulled a section of the paper towards me.

"*Garfield's* funny, isn't he?" I said. "Look at this one. Poor Jon; he tries so hard to date the vet."

"Are you searching for jobs or not?"

"Okay. I'll take a look. After I've read *Peanuts.*"

Fiona rolled her eyes and ran her pen down a column of small advertisements.

"Here's one," she said. "Administration assistant required in central Christchurch."

"That's a step down from your employment in London, isn't it?"

"I can't afford to be choosy. Oh. They require ten years' experience. I only have two."

"Ten years as an administration assistant? They don't want people with ambition, do they?"

"Here's another job I could do. Receptionist needed. 8:00 a.m. to 6:00 p.m., Monday to Friday. I'll give them a ring. It's an agency."

Fiona circled the advertisement and turned the page.

I sighed and studied the section she'd discarded.

"Paint salesman," I said. "I could do that."

"You've never worked in a paint shop."

"I've worked in sales. The skills must be transferable."

"What salary are they paying?"

"Doesn't say."

I tore out the vacancy and folded it in half.

Fiona highlighted two more advertisements.

She picked up the phone. "I'm going to call these agencies. I'll see if I can set something up for next week."

"All right. I'm just going for a pee."

I opened the front door and crossed the porch to the wash house.

Phillip rode past on his motorbike. He waved.

A horse whinnied.

Jazz rubbed his nose against my leg. He sat and waited for my invitation to ask him to hop on the four-wheel bike or round up some cows.

I ruffled his ears and stared across the farmyard at the milking shed.

Fiona replaced the phone handset as I returned.

"I've spoken to an agency, and they want me to come in for a typing test tomorrow."

"Tomorrow? We can't go to Christchurch tomorrow. Phillip's teaching me how to bale silage."

"I'm sure he'll manage without you. He's going to have to now. Could you please find those CVs we printed? I think they're in the top of the backpack."

My mouth turned down, and I poked out my bottom lip.

Fiona hugged me, then stepped back.

"You can't be a farmer for ever. You'll have to return to reality at some point."

≈≈≈

The bus to Christchurch wound through the mountains and stopped briefly at Arthur's Pass village.

"I wish we'd found a seat near the front," said Fiona. "I feel sick."

"We're over the pass. That's the worst of it behind us."

Fiona doubled her coat over and shoved it against the window. She closed her eyes.

I leant into the aisle and stared through the windscreen past rows of other passengers. We bumped across the sex bridge. The effect wasn't the same as in Linda's car.

The driver sped up, and the vehicle entered the long, straight Canterbury plains.

Take Me Home, Country Roads. But they're taking me away from home. Away from the West Coast. Away from the farm.

Auntie Debbie welcomed us at the front door of her suburban house.

"How would you be?" she said. "Did you have a pleasant trip?"

Her fluffy, blonde hair draped over her shoulders. I noticed she wore bedroom slippers, as if she were about to audition for *Coronation Street*.

"Thanks for having us," said Fiona. "We'll try not to be a nuisance."

"Pop your bag in the spare bedroom," said Debbie. "It's barbecue tonight, is that okay?"

"Yum," said Fiona. "I'll help you prepare it."

The Christchurch Press lay unfolded on Debbie's dining room table. I scrutinized the job page, while Fiona and Debbie chopped salad and discussed life in Hokitika.

What can I do? I don't want to work in an office again. I enjoy farming.

An advertisement caught my eye. 'Farm machinery sales representative wanted. Must be familiar with Massey Ferguson.'

"There's a job here I'd be good at. Tractor salesman."

Fiona and Debbie both laughed.

"I didn't realise those jobs existed," said Debbie, "I thought the farmers just went to the dealership and bought them."

"You've never sold tractors," said Fiona.

"I've driven tractors," I said. "The advertisement says they want someone who's familiar with Massey Ferguson. Your dad's tractors are all Massey Ferguson."

"Give it a go," said Debbie. "You don't know unless you try."

"May I use your phone please, Debbie?"

"Of course. It's in the hall."

I held the newspaper in front of me and dialled.

"Hello, is that Harrison's Farm Machinery? I'm calling about the sales job advertised in the Christchurch Press. Yes, I'm familiar with Massey Ferguson. Yes, I'll bring a copy of my CV. Tomorrow at 10:00 a.m.? All right, thank you."

I replaced the phone, pushed open the kitchen door, and grinned.

"They've offered me an interview. They want me to come in tomorrow."

"That's fantastic," said Fiona. "Did you bring your suit?"

"Do I need a suit to sell tractors?"

"You'd better dress smartly for an interview."

"I'll see what we can find in the wardrobe," said Debbie. "There'll be something that'll fit you. I'll open a bottle of wine with dinner, to celebrate."

"Erm, okay," I said. "They haven't given me the job yet."

The managing director of Harrison's Farm Machinery perused my CV, as I sat opposite him. The Toblerone-shaped nameplate on his desk identified him as John Bryant, so whoever Harrison was, it wasn't him.

I watched him read and shuffled in my seat.

John looked up at me.

"You've no experience at all selling tractors. I thought you said on the phone you were familiar with Massey Ferguson?"

He propped his chin on his hands and challenged me to respond.

"I'm experienced in sales, and I've been working on my girlfriend's father's farm on the West Coast. He owns Massey Fergusons, and I drive them. Your farming customers will appreciate a salesman with a real-world agricultural background."

"Hmmm."

He flipped my CV over and back, pulled the arm of his glasses so they slid down his nose, and inspected me over them.

"What models do they have on your farm, Simon?"

"Erm, the little tractor's a model 55."

John laughed. "Model 55? I think there's one of those in the Christchurch Museum."

"There are two newer ones as well," I said. "The one with the loader's a model 174. We own the four-wheel drive option. The 174—4."

That bit of technical information should impress you.

"Gees," said John. He laughed again. "We're getting more recent. But I haven't seen that model for years."

"And," I said, "the cab tractor's a model 275."

"Is that it?" said John. "The newest tractor's a ten-year-old 275?"

"Err, yes."

I felt my face tingle.

"Have you ever operated a model 6150, or an 8130?" asked John.

I allowed my agricultural education had omitted these particular denominations.

John added my CV to a pile of papers on his desk and pushed his chair back.

"Thanks for coming in, Simon. I've had several applications for the vacancy. We'll be in touch."

I stood and shook his hand.

"Thanks John, I hope to hear from you."

He held the door open and gave me an odd look.

≈≈≈

"How'd it go, Simon?" asked Debbie.

I took off the suit jacket and hung it up.

"Erm, not too well. I think they want someone with more industry experience. Where's Fiona?"

"She went to an interview in the city. Ah, here she is."

The front door closed, and Fiona entered, in attire I hadn't seen her wearing since we'd lived in London.

"Good interview?" I asked.

She hung up her raincoat.

"At first it went well," she said. "I found the agency, I took a typing test, and they sent me directly to a company advertising for an administrator."

"Wow," I said, "that's good."

"Anyway," said Fiona, "while I waited in reception, I studied some company literature I found there, so I could glean some information about their products."

"Yep, good move," I said. "It impresses interviewers if you show industry knowledge."

"After a few minutes, a door opened, and three men wearing suits waited to see me. We discussed my experience, then one of them asked whether I had any queries. I opened the company brochure I'd found and posed what I thought were intelligent questions about the products they made, and the major industries forming their customer base."

"Sounds perfect."

Her shoulders slumped.

"It wasn't. They were so condescending. One of the interviewers said, "you're a bit of a detective, aren't you, for a young girl?" He turned to the next page of my CV, saw the details of Dad's policeman friend who's one of my referees, laughed, and said, 'ah yes, here we are, Detective Rex Bassett.' I felt so humiliated. An interviewer in London would never have spoken to me in that fashion."

I wrapped my arms around her.

She shrugged and pulled off her high heels. "How was your interview at the tractor place?"

"I'm not sure my knowledge of farm machinery's recent enough," I said. "I think they want someone who's done the exact job before."

"Keep trying," said Debbie. "Early days yet."

≈≈≈

I tipped cereal into a bowl and watched diagonal precipitation drift across Debbie's garden. I couldn't fathom why the West Coast suffered such a reputation for rain. I'd seen more wet days in Christchurch.

Garfield conversed with a spider on page 47 of the newspaper. The farm machinery dealer hadn't called, so I filed my bowl and spoon in the dishwasher and pulled a cutting from my pocket.

"Hello, is that Canterbury paint shop? Are you still looking for a salesman? I've about four years' sales experience, and I can start any day. Great, I'll see you this afternoon at 2:00 p.m."

My heart sped up, as I walked along the single-storey row of shops, searching for number twelve.

I hesitated outside the double-fronted paint store. The window display comprised stacks of colourful tins, and for some reason a life-size cardboard cut-out of Rolf Harris gazed benevolently at passers-by.

I took a deep breath, pushed the door handle, and heard a bell tinkle. A small man in a flat cap and dark-brown overalls contemplated me from behind a counter.

I was in the Two Ronnies' *Four Candles* sketch.

"Hello," I said, "I'm here for a job interview."

"Right-o," said the man, "head through to the back."

He pointed with his thumb and lifted a hatch in the countertop. I walked under it and entered a windowless room with classroom-like chairs arranged around the walls. A man of about thirty years old sat in one of them and watched me enter.

He nodded awkwardly. We were both here for the same thing and we were competitors. We weren't friends.

I sat and held my CV.

Voices behind a translucent glass door became louder. The door opened and revealed a plump, middle-aged man. He shook a young lady's hand. He wore a white shirt with the sleeves rolled up to the elbows, and ellipses of bare tummy peeked between the lower buttons.

"Thanks for coming, Sharon. We'll be in touch." He surveyed the room. "Next, please."

My competitor stood up, offered the shirt-sleeved man his hand to shake, and entered the office. The door closed and muffled their speech.

I gazed around the room's museum-like exhibition of paint marketing collateral, as the butterflies in my stomach began a complicated square-dancing routine.

Various vintages of Rolf Harris's goatee-bearded face beamed from posters and posed with tins of a brand called British Paints. I wondered if I was supposed to be familiar with the make. I'd never seen it in England.

I studied the posters and ruminated on the concept of a New Zealand paint store, selling a brand of paint named for Britain, advertised by an Australian television personality.

The door opened, and the previous applicant departed. I sucked in a breath and stood up.

"Good afternoon, I'm Brian," said the shirt-sleeved man. "Thanks for coming in."

I shook his hand.

"I'm Simon," I said. "Pleased to meet you."

"Oh," said Brian. "The last chap's name was Simon, too. What a coincidence."

Please don't confuse us. Just because he's got the same name as me doesn't mean he's as strong a candidate for the job.

Brian picked up a pair of spectacles by one arm and flicked them open.

He perched them on the end of his nose, ran his hand through his thinning hair, and perused my application.

I heard a clock tick, and felt my heart beat.

He placed my CV in front of him, propped his elbows on the desk, laid his chin on his folded hands, and examined me.

"So, Simon, you've worked in sales in London for four years?" His black Hitler moustache wiggled as he spoke.

"Yes, Brian. Print and packaging. A similar industry to paint."

"I'm sure," said Brian. "What do you know about paint?"

"I note you carry a few different makes. British Paints, courtesy of television personality Rolf Harris, as well as Dulux, and Wattle."

"Very good," said Brian. "Rolf's one of the most popular entertainers in the world right now. He's advertised British Paints for twenty years, since the 1970s. But which brand d'you reckon's the best seller?"

Oh no. This must be a trick question. Deep breath. Here we go.

"British Paints?"

"Nope," said Brian. "Dulux. Outsells the others two-to-one."

First initiative test failed.

"What compensation were you hoping for?" asked Brian.

"Erm, I've recently arrived in New Zealand, and I'm not familiar with the salaries here. In England I earnt the equivalent of one thousand dollars a week."

"Hmm. We can only offer nine-fifty for this job."

"Nine hundred and fifty dollars a week. That'll be okay. It's close to what I took home in London."

"Not nine hundred and fifty dollars a week," said Brian. "Nine-fifty. Nine dollars, fifty cents an hour."

My lips pressed together. Fiona and I needed to be self-sufficient. Not depend on relatives like kind Auntie Debbie for charity. We'd never be independent on that wage.

"D'you have any other questions for me, Simon?"

"I think that's all, Brian. Thanks for seeing me."

"No problem, we'll let you know."

He stood up, shook my hand, and opened the door, revealing two more candidates.

Rolf Harris grinned at me as I departed.

Fiona looked at the pavement and shook her head.

"I've suffered the worst day ever," she said, as we sheltered from driving rain at a bus stop. "I attended an agency appointment, they sent me straight to a job, and when I arrived there'd been a stuff-up, and the company had already filled the vacancy. Another agency made me wait for an hour, and then told me I didn't have enough experience. It made me so angry. I might be 22 years old, but I worked as a director's personal assistant in London for over a year; I can do this reception and administration work in my sleep. I hate this job seeking. And there isn't any temp work like in England."

She paused. I watched the bus approach in the distance.

"Anyway, tell me about the paint store," she said. "How d'you think you did?"

"Not sure," I said. "There were several applicants. And the money's not great. I don't think they'll offer it to me."

The bus stopped, and the doors opened. Fiona ruffled her umbrella, and we boarded for the ride back to Debbie's house.

"D'you have any other interviews lined up?" I asked.

"Nope," said Fiona. "You?"

"None," I said. "Why don't we go home?"

Fiona grinned and her eyes lit up. "Home? Back to London?"

15. ARTHUR DALEY

"We can't return to London," I said. "The reason we moved to New Zealand is because your British visa expired, didn't it? I mean, let's go back to the farm for the weekend."

"Oh. Okay. The farm. Sure. I'll ring up and book the bus tickets."

The number 86 pulled away, and I watched the raindrops dribble down the window.

≈≈≈

"Your brother called," said Debbie, as Fiona hung up her coat.

"Which brother?"

"Colin. He rang from his work at Honda. A customer traded in a car today, and he wondered if you'd be interested in it. He said it's about thirteen years old, but it's an excellent runner."

"What d'you reckon, Fiona?" I said. "We need a car."

"Yep. I'm sick of standing in the rain waiting for buses. I wonder how much money they're asking for it? Can I use the phone, Deb?"

"Of course."

Fiona dialled while I mulled over our financial situation. Thanks to the kindness of Fiona's parents, living in Hokitika cost little. I hoped my efforts at farm work repaid them, even with all my mistakes. But our savings were nearly extinguished. If we didn't find employment soon, we'd be broke.

Fiona returned to the kitchen.

"The car's seven thousand dollars. I told Colin we couldn't afford it but then he…"

"Seven thousand dollars?" I said, "for a thirteen-year-old Honda? Does it have gold-plated tyres?"

113

"Let me finish. I told him we couldn't afford it, and he reminded me; ten years ago, we all received shares from the meat company where Dad's on the board. If I sell those shares, we can buy the car. Colin will allow us to test drive it over the weekend, and we can pay him later."

"I hope they can negotiate on the price," I said. "Are you sure you want to cash in the shares?"

"I'd forgotten I owned them. I'll call Dad and ask him how I sell."

≈≈≈

A row of gleaming Hondas stood on the white floor, their doors and boots open, enticing me to investigate them and fiddle with as many controls as I felt necessary.

Fiona approached the receptionist.

I opened the door of a family saloon, plopped behind the wheel, and examined the multiple compartments and cubby-holes.

Fiona returned and sat in the passenger seat.

"Look," I said, reaching above my head. "This Honda Accord has a place to keep your sunglasses."

Fiona inhaled through her nose. "I love the brand-new-car smell. I wish you could buy it in bottles."

A man in a white coat poked his head through the window.

"G'day, Col," said Fiona. "Long time, no see."

I reckoned Colin was the same age as me. He ran his hand through his short, brown hair, and grinned.

We stepped out. Fiona hugged him, and I shook his hand.

Fiona gazed around the showroom.

The polished tiles reflected stark ceiling lighting.

"Which one of these is it?" she asked.

"None of them," said Colin. "Your car's around the back."

We followed him through a door marked 'workshop'.

Colin selected some keys from a rack and led us to an outdoor area crammed with cars of assorted makes and vintages. A young man walked between them squirting a spray and rubbing the bodywork with a cloth.

"Here's yours," said Colin. He placed his hand on the bonnet of a blue, two-door sports car.

"1983 Honda Prelude. Great runner, full service history and only one lady owner," said Colin, doing his best Arthur Daley impersonation. "You won't have any trouble with this."

I ran my hand over discoloured paint on the bonnet.

"We'll take it," said Fiona.

Hang on. I haven't started bargaining yet.

I lay down on the concrete and inspected the underside. I wasn't sure what I hoped to achieve by this, but I completed my scrutiny by standing, shaking my head, and sucking in through my clenched teeth.

"There's nothing wrong with the bodywork," said Colin. "Cars in Christchurch don't rust."

I opened the boot and lifted its base.

"The spare tyre's missing."

"We'll find you a spare," said Colin. "There'll be one in the workshop."

I sat in the car and turned the key. The engine started immediately. I revved the throttle, switched on the lights and the indicators, opened the glove box, and pulled out the ashtray.

"Stop playing with the car, and let's do the paperwork," said Fiona. "Colin'll help us if there are any issues. He's a mechanic, remember?"

I turned the engine off and watched Fiona and Colin disappear into the showroom.

≈≈≈

"At least the windscreen wipers work," said Fiona, as drizzle hid the mountains.

We waited for a Trans-West Freighters truck to cross the sex bridge. The driver waved as he accelerated past.

Fiona giggled. "Let's see how she handles this," she said. "Ready?"

"She?"

"All cars are shes."

Her hands gripped the wheel, and she shuffled her bottom on the seat.

We bounced over the familiar rhythm.

"Pretty good," said Fiona. "Better than Mum's car."

"Can we stop in Arthur's Pass village?" I asked. "I need a pee."

"Sure," said Fiona. "Then you can have a drive."

"What, through the one-way zig-zaggy bit?"

"Yep. I've crossed the pass hundreds of times. I've been driving since I turned fifteen, remember? I'll talk you through it."

Fiona stopped outside the Arthur's Pass café, and I ran for the bathroom.

When I returned, I paused and watched Fiona lean against the passenger door and stare at the mountain tops. The rain had cleared, and a brisk breeze blew her dark-red hair across her face.

She's so gorgeous. She could advertise New Zealand tourism. Or Honda cars.

Fiona turned around and smiled. "Ready?" she said.

I sat in the driver's seat, gripped the wheel, adjusted the seat and mirrors, and pulled out.

The road wound up the mountain pass. Ahead, I glimpsed the blue of a West Coast summer's day.

"Where's all this Westland rain people talk about?"

"The Coast has a worse reputation than the reality," said Fiona.

Left bend.

Right bend.

Death's Corner.

Grim Reaper still absent.

Fiona leant towards me and peered between the steering wheel spokes.

"You can drive faster. We're only going fifteen kilometres per hour."

I blinked. "I'm being careful. New car; unfamiliar, windy road."

"Yes, but I think Trans-West Freighters wants to pass you."

I glanced in my rear-view mirror and discovered it contained a truck's flat bonnet.

"He sneaked up suddenly," I said. "He'll have to wait. He can't overtake me here."

I stopped at the apex of the single-lane precipice, the vertical cliff on my right, and the sheer drop to my left.

"You can't stop," said Fiona. "You're in the middle of the road."

I edged down the hill and pumped the brake to arrest my descent.

Trans-West changed gear three millimetres behind me.

We approached the tunnel, as a campervan entered it, heading up the mountain road.

"Remind me, whose right of way is it?"

"His. Wait here. You're going downhill; he needs the momentum."

I heard the sneeze of Trans-West Freighter's air brakes. If the truck came any closer to my rear bumper he'd be an integral part of our car.

The campervan passed us. The blond Teutonic driver grasped his wheel and stared over the dashboard, his mouth in a straight line. My mirror offered the view of his tail inching around the bend.

I released the brake and continued. Trans-West Freighters followed, and I sped up to escape his bonnet.

"Are you in gear?" asked Fiona.

"Nope, I'm coasting downhill in neutral. It saves petrol."

"You'd better ask Dad for some driving lessons. There's a big difference between country driving and city driving. Dad always taught me to put the car in low gear coming down the mountain. Then there's less chance of her running away from you."

I engaged third. The engine screamed and attempted to climb out of the bonnet.

"There," said Fiona. "The gears are helping you brake now."

I've so much to learn still.

$$\approx\approx\approx$$

"..it's another stunning West Coast day with an overnight low of eleven degrees. We'll be right back with Cutting Crew and '(I Just) Died in Your Arms' after we go to Patricia on the news desk. Stay tuned to 93.1 Scenicland FM."

A plume of gravel dust followed us down the driveway. I parked, opened the door, and smelt the familiar scent of cow.

Jazz sprinted up to me. His tail wagged, and he rubbed his nose against my knee.

I crouched down, stroked his head, and smiled.

"No-one's here," said Fiona.

She opened the garden gate and fingered the corner of a double sheet, flapping in the breeze.

"The washing's dry. I'll bring it in."

"I'll give the grass a cut," I said. "The lawn's getting long."

I smiled to myself and changed into my farming clothes.

≈≈≈

Phillip pulled up on his motorbike, and I turned off the mower.

"Hello, Simon," he said. "Nice car. How was Christchurch? Did you find a job?"

"Hi, Phillip. Not yet. I've been to a couple of interviews. One at a paint shop and one as a tractor salesman."

"How did the tractor one go?" He grinned. "Were they impressed with your farming knowledge?"

"I told them about our Massey Fergusons, and the interviewer laughed at me. He couldn't believe our newest tractor's ten years old."

"They farm on a different scale over there," said Phillip. "They have bigger, more modern operations with irrigation systems. Instead of herringbone milking sheds they have rotaries."

"What's a rotary?"

"The herd stands on a turntable facing the middle. Farmers work in a channel on the outside, and the animals rotate past them. All the cows move, not the staff."

"Wow. I'd love to see one of those. How many cows can they fit on the turntable at once?"

"My friend owns a 44-stall shed."

"Forty-four cows? He can milk the entire herd in five rotations?"

"Some of those farms on the east coast have two thousand cows. They process them in shifts, day and night."

"Gosh. I thought our farm was big."

"Anyway, it's time for milking," said Phillip. "D'you want to fetch the cows? I'll start the machine."

I grinned, summoned Jazz, and ran to the four-wheel bike.

≈≈≈

The big Massey Ferguson 275 bumped around the paddock, negotiating small clumps of trees and tracking along the creek banks, as I cut another field for silage, the cows' food when winter temperatures arrested the growth of the grass.

A single cloud hung in another perfect sky, as blue as the American Express logo. This West Coast rain, I concluded, was a myth perpetuated by locals who didn't want outsiders to discover their scenic paradise.

I drove the tractor back to the farmyard, kicked off my boots, and entered the kitchen door.

Fiona studied the Christchurch newspaper. She drew a picture of a tree in the margin and shaded it in.

"Any new jobs?" I asked.

"Nothing today," she said. "D'you want to go to the pub? My brother Graeme played with the local rugby team this afternoon; Mum and Dad have gone to the after-match drinks."

"Sure. I could do with a cold beer. It's boiling in the cab, driving up and down the fields all day."

Fiona switched the car blower onto full speed and wound down the windows. Her hair waved behind her, as if she were Bonnie Tyler in a 1980s rock video.

She turned a corner, slowed down, and entered the pub car park.

Something didn't look right.

I froze and ducked down in the footwell.

"Quick, turn around!" I said. "Get us out of here. We need to call the police. There's a man with a gun."

16. MATHEMATICAL BEER

Cold sweat ran down my forehead. I hid under the glove box and jabbed my finger above my head.

Fiona laughed and parked the car between two others.

"Fiona, get down. There's a man in the car park with a shotgun. We have to call the cops. Why are you laughing?"

"It's just a farmer storing his gun in the boot of his car. He'll have been shooting rabbits. It's perfectly normal."

I peeked above the dashboard.

"It's not perfectly normal to see a man wielding a shotgun in a pub car park where I come from."

"Ssh. I don't want people to think you're a townie. Come on, let's buy a drink."

The armed offender slammed his boot, removed his flat cap, and scratched his head. I gave him a hard stare Paddington Bear would have been proud of.

The door to the white, wooden pub contained a small boy clad in green shorts and red Wellington boots, holding a bag of Bluebird potato crisps. He ran into the pub ahead of me. An older man ruffled his hair and passed him a lemonade bottle.

The smells of beer and sweat entered my nostrils. Groups of farming-clothed people stood chatting, all holding glasses of assorted liquids. I recognised Fiona's grandfather in the far corner conversing with men of a similar age. Children ran around the adults' legs, laughing and crushing salted peanuts into the orange-and-brown patterned carpet.

I liked this scene.

One farming valley.

One community.

One pub at the centre.

121

Frank and Linda stood with a young man wearing a soiled, collared jersey, with smears of mud across his face, as if he'd recently completed army camouflage training.

"This is my youngest brother, Graeme," said Fiona.

"G'day, Simon," said Graeme. "These country folk treating you right? Has Frank got you betting on the gee-gees yet?"

His legs had green grass stains which were duplicated on his navy shorts, and he wore thick woollen socks without shoes.

"Getting on well, thanks, Graeme. Nice to meet you."

"That's the way," he said.

"Let me buy some drinks," I said. "What'll you have?"

Frank studied his empty glass. "I'll have a seven of CD, please."

"A twelve of DB, thanks," said Graeme.

This appeared to be a rather mathematical way of ordering beer. I wondered if I should request a nine of AB for myself.

"A white wine, please," said Linda.

I waited behind three men, wearing checked shirts, who perched on bar stools. They conversed with the barman and collected a round of beer in egg cup-sized glasses.

"I don't understand what I'm supposed to order," I whispered to Fiona. "I'm used to pints and half-pints. What are all these numbers and letters?"

She laughed. "Beer's sold in sevens and twelves here. It's the quantity of ounces in the glass."

"Right. Seven's a half-pint, and twelve's a pint?"

"Bit smaller. Those guys are drinking sevens."

"Okay, and what's DB?"

"DB's a beer. It stands for Dominion Breweries."

"And the other one? CD, I think your dad said."

"CD's a beer too. Canterbury Draught."

"Right. And what would you like?"

Fiona grinned. "I'll have an L&P."

"You're winding me up. There isn't a drink called L&P."

"Lemon and Paeroa," she said. "It's a New Zealand soft-drink."

"Right. A seven of CD, a twelve of DB and an L&P. And your mum wants a white wine. Am I supposed to ask for a WW?"

The checked-shirted men picked up their beers. They left piles of coins and notes on the bar.

I called after them.

"Excuse me, you forgot your change?"

One man turned around and gave me an odd look.

The landlord leant over the bar on his outstretched hands.

"G'day, Simon. I'm Gary. What can I serve you?"

A mop of straight hair framed his ruddy face, and the tips of his walrus moustache moved as he spoke.

How does he know my name?

"Hi, Gary. I hope I remember this correctly. Could I have a seven of CD, a twelve of DB, and an L&P? Oh, and a white wine."

"No problem, Simon."

Gary upended some glasses and filled them from the beer taps. He cracked open a brown-and-yellow soft-drink can and set it down on the bar, next to an empty tumbler. He opened a glass-fronted fridge, removed a wine bottle, and poured it into a tall glass.

"Anything else?"

One, two, three, four. Who have I forgotten? Oh, yes, me.

"Um, I don't suppose you sell Boddington's?"

"Bonnington's? Isn't that cough syrup?"

"It's a beer from England. Never mind." I studied the taps and selected one. "I'll have a Monteith's please. A twelve."

At least Monteith's isn't ordered as an acronym.

I distributed the drinks and pointed at the pub counter.

"Linda, those men forgot their change. They left it on the bar."

She laughed. "All the regulars put their coins near their usual stool. When they order another drink, Gary subtracts the amount from their pile. At the end of the night, he clears the money away, and puts the coins in containers with people's names on them."

She pointed to a row of white tins behind the bar, with black writing scrawled on each one: 'Geoff', 'Bob', 'Mick', 'Cheryl'.

"But won't someone walk off with their money?"

"Not around here, Simon. You're not in London now."

Fiona took my arm. "Come with me. There's an animal I want to show you."

"An animal? In a pub?"

She led me to a glass case. It contained an evil-looking stuffed mammal with pointy yellow teeth. The taxidermist had posed it standing up, leaning against a twig, holding a toy pop-gun, like Elmer Fudd taking aim at Bugs Bunny.

"What's that?" I asked.

"Remember the night up at Fox River when those animal sounds kept you awake?"

"Yes, my hair stands on end thinking about it."

"This creature made the noises."

"This is a possum?"

"Yep."

"Gosh. I thought they'd be bigger. They sound bigger. Next time I hear them I won't be so scared."

I toasted the possum and returned to the conversation.

≈≈≈

Fiona circled jobs in the classifieds.

"There are a couple of new vacancies today," she said. "I'll make some phone calls this afternoon."

"Are we going back to Christchurch?" I asked.

"If I schedule an interview," said Fiona. She smiled. "Or if you do."

"I don't want to live in Christchurch. I like it here."

"We can't stay here with no income. And farm work's a novelty; you'll become bored with it."

"I'm not bored yet. See you soon, I'm going to the shed to help Phillip."

The last two rows of cows stood with their milking cups attached to their udders. I studied the egg-shaped sight-glasses and tried to identify which one would need removing first.

"D'you want to finish up in here?" asked Phillip. "I'll wash the yard."

He stepped out of the concrete channel into the area where the cows queued to be milked. I heard the splash of water from the big hose.

Twenty-four cows.

Twenty-four sets of milking cups to be removed.

In the right order.

I marched along the trench.

I watched the milk spurt through the sight glasses.

Squirt, splash, squirt, splash.

Two showed fresh air. I removed their milking cups and hung them up.

I could hear the hose, but I couldn't see Phillip.

I took more sets off, until all the cups on one side were hung up.

I opened the gate. Twelve cows walked out.

The final cows on the other side finished. I removed their cups and released them.

I've completed the milking.

By myself.

"Phillip, we're done. That's the last cows."

He turned off the hose.

"Good job, Simon," he said. "Did you remember to spray the udders?"

I turned around and noticed the bottle.

"Oh, no. Sorry, I forgot. Should I run around the paddock and squirt them now?"

Phillip laughed.

"It'll be okay. So long as they're treated tomorrow. D'you want to lock them in for the night?"

He turned the hose back on. I walked out to find Jazz and the four-wheel bike.

≈≈≈

"Frank, I finished the milking today. Phillip wasn't watching. I did it by myself."

"Isn't that marvellous?" said Frank. "You'll be running the show soon."

"You had a phone call while you were out," said Fiona.

"A phone call? Who would ring me?"

"Colin. On his way home from work he noticed a sandwich board. He said the Toyota dealer has a vacancy for a car detailer."

"What's a car detailer?"

"Someone who washes cars to prepare them for sale and keeps them polished. Like the chap we saw at Honda when we collected our car."

"That job doesn't sound challenging. I can't imagine it would pay any more than the paint shop."

"You don't have a job at all," said Fiona. "You can't be picky."

The phone rang.

"That'll be Colin again," said Fiona.

I winked and answered it in my poshest English accent. "Wall family residence. Chief butler speaking."

A lady's voice laughed. "Hello, could I speak with Fiona, please?"

"Certainly. I'll put her on."

I overheard one end of the conversation.

"Hello, this is Fiona. Yes, that's right. Tomorrow at two? Great, see you then."

Fiona turned to me.

"We're going back to Christchurch. Office Professionals want to interview me. You'd better ring Colin and find out more details about the Toyota job."

≈≈≈

The young receptionist at the Toyota dealership smiled, as I strode across her showroom in my borrowed suit. She revealed teeth a dentist's waiting-room poster would have been proud of.

"Good morning, sir. Were you requiring sales or service?"

Her immaculate make-up shone in the harsh lights under her long, straight, bleached-blonde hair.

I held out my hand.

"I'm here about the car detailing job."

"Oh."

She regarded me as if she'd discovered a possum turd on her white-tiled floor.

"Take a seat. I'll page the workshop manager."

She spoke into a microphone mounted on her desk.

"Mark, to reception please. Mark, to reception."

She returned to her computer.

A dark-haired, middle-aged man dressed in white overalls strode through a rear door.

The receptionist pointed. "Another one about the job."

Another one? Oh dear.

I stood up.

"Yes?" said the man. He didn't introduce himself.

I smiled and held out my hand.

"Hi, Mark, is it? I'm Simon. I'm here about the car detailing role you're advertising on the sign outside."

He wiped his hands on a cloth.

"D'you have a CV?"

"Erm, not with me. I didn't realise I'd need one for this."

"I see. How many years' experience d'you have?"

Years' experience? How hard is it to wash a car?

"I haven't detailed cars before," I said, "but I'm a quick learner."

"I'm sure you are. Come back with your CV and leave it with Bridget. I've received about 150 applications, so don't get your hopes up."

My shoulders dropped.

"Okay, thanks Mark, I will."

Mark turned to the receptionist. "Is Mr Shannon coming to collect his Corolla today? He said he'd be here first thing."

"I'll call him," she said.

She picked up the phone. Mark flicked through some paperwork on her desk.

Nobody noticed me leave.

I ran through a light shower of rain and joined Fiona, as she sheltered in a shop doorway.

"How'd it go today," I asked her, "with the office agency?"

"I took a typing test which I passed, they asked me a few questions about my experience, and said they'd be in touch. It's so annoying, I don't think they have any vacancies, they're just collecting resumés. How d'you get on at Toyota?"

"What a waste of time. They've received 150 applications for a job washing cars, and they wanted to know how many years' experience I had. It's crazy. Do people do these types of jobs as careers here? I knew it'd be different to London, but I didn't realise how different."

A squall of wind snowed leaves from the trees. They blew around the pavement in a mini-whirlwind and settled against a pair of telephone boxes.

Fiona shivered. She pulled the car keys out of her handbag.

"Come on. Let's go back to Debbie's."

≈≈≈

"Someone rang while you were out," said Debbie.

Fiona closed the front door and pulled off her high heels.

"Another agency, I suppose."

She put the car keys on a shelf and hung up her coat.

"Nope," said Debbie, "it was your mum. Call her back. She said she's got some exciting news."

17. HUHU

I cleaned our car, while Fiona rang Linda. I reckoned I should practise, in case the other 150 applicants for the Toyota job all dropped dead.

Fiona walked out of the house and sat on Debbie's front doorstep.

She watched me and grinned.

I raised my eyebrows at her and plopped my cloth into a bucket.

"What are you smiling about?" I asked.

"Someone's offered me a job."

"Seriously? I thought you called your mum."

"I did. She told me her friend's husband needs an accounts clerk at his hardware shop. They've known me all my life; I won't have to be interviewed or anything."

"Can you do accounts?"

"Of course. I worked in accounts for a year in London before my promotion to personal assistant."

"Wow. Great. Whereabouts in Christchurch is the store located?"

Fiona held both my hands. Her eyes sparkled and her mouth stretched so wide I thought it would run out of face.

"You'll like this, Simon."

I clenched my teeth.

"Come on, tell me. Don't keep me in suspense."

She squeezed my hands.

"The job's in Hokitika. We're going home."

"..it's going to be a perfect day for this weekend's exciting activities. We hope to see you for the big event at Cass Square, but whatever you're doing, keep your radio tuned to 93.1 Scenicland FM. And now 'Broken Wings' by.."

I turned off the car and inhaled the familiar scent of farm. Jazz ran up to me, sneezed, and rubbed his head on my trousers. I ruffled his woolly, black ears. A gentle breeze blew white clouds across the pale, blue sky, as I whistled '*Home, Home on the Range*'.

The milking machine hummed, and I watched a line of cows stroll along a track to their new pasture.

I put my hands on my hips and smiled.

"Frank," shouted Linda, "clear up that mess before someone trips over and breaks a leg."

A toolbox had exploded over the lawn. Two sawhorses stood next to the washing line, and a deep layer of wood shavings buried the surrounding grass, as if a miniature local volcano had erupted in the front garden. A saw, a hammer, and a box of nails lay half-buried.

The rear end of Frank protruded from a ground-level hole in a wooden building.

I walked over and addressed Frank's bottom.

"G'day, Frank. Need any help?"

Frank reversed out of the hole and stood up.

His hair scattered sawdust like the 'before' picture in a Vosene anti-dandruff advert.

"You're going to need somewhere to live if you're staying here, so I'd better repair this workers' hut. It's not a large home, but it'll give you two a bit of independence."

He brushed wood shavings off his jumper.

"Thanks, Frank. Wow. I'm so glad we'll be living on the farm. I didn't want to stay in Christchurch."

Frank nodded. "Country life does provide a variety of dimensions."

He picked up his hammer and re-entered the hole.

I stumped off to help Phillip finish the evening milking.

≈≈≈

"You're home in time for the Wild Foods Festival," said Linda, as she pulled a packet of Nutrigrain cereal out of the pantry.

"Wild Foods Festival?" I asked.

I had a vision of angry fish fingers, running around a stage, waving cocktail sticks.

"It's the West Coast's biggest event of the year," said Fiona. "Thousands of people descend on us from all over New Zealand. The town's population triples for the weekend."

"Is it a rock concert?"

"There'll be bands there, but the festival's all about the food."

"Sounds good," I said. I licked my lips. "What sort of things can you buy?"

"Last year," said Angela, "I ate fried grasshoppers, snails, and pig's snouts. Apparently, this year you'll be able to try lambs' testicles."

"Hilarious," I said.

She smiled and raised her eyebrows.

I turned to Linda.

"Tell me she's joking."

"Some local people started the Wild Foods Festival a few years ago as a bit of a laugh," said Linda. "They intended to recreate the pioneer days of Hokitika and serve up the bush food the early gold miners might have gathered to survive. It's diversified from that original concept; I'm fairly certain Victorian miners didn't eat lambs' testicles."

I frowned. "Erm, is there any normal food to eat?"

"I'm sure there'll be something more palatable to your townie tastes, city boy," said Angela.

In case there wasn't, I poured an extra bowl of Nutrigrain and shovelled it into my mouth.

Linda gazed out of the window and then inspected Angela, Fiona, and me.

"Have you three applied sunscreen this morning? Put some on," she said. "There isn't much shade at the festival. The sun'll burn you to a crisp."

Fiona's grandfather manned the gate, under a white gazebo advertising Lions' Clubs International.

"Hi, Pop," said Fiona.

"Have you brought your young man to try some of our local delicacies?" he asked. He winked and tore off four tickets.

We entered the first tent.

"You'll enjoy these," said Linda. "Something tame to start."

A lady in a white apron stood behind a trestle table covered in a white paper cloth. She brandished a piece of meat on a skewer.

"Would you like to try a sample of possum sausage?"

"Hi, Joan," Linda said to the vendor. "We're introducing Simon to West Coast food."

I pulled the meat off the skewer. It felt warm and greasy.

"Thanks," I said. I bit off a small piece.

"Can I have some?" asked Fiona.

I passed her the rest of the portion.

"I'll take two of those, thanks," I said to Joan.

I turned to Fiona. She chewed her possum.

"What do you think?"

"It's a strong meat, isn't it? Gamey. I don't think I could eat a lot."

I divided my purchase between the four of us, and we continued.

"Bleeeurgghh," said Linda. She navigated around the next tent and stood some distance away.

"Lambs brains," said Fiona. "Mum can't stand the smell of lamb cooking."

I observed a man stirring a roundabout-sized frying pan piled with light-coloured mince.

"D'you want some brains?" he asked. He offered me a morsel on a plastic spoon.

The sample of brains smelt of lamb.

The sample of brains tasted of lamb, which was slightly disappointing.

I shrugged.

We caught up with Linda and Angela at the next stall. They both clenched something in a napkin which looked familiar, but out of place.

"Chicken's foot, Simon?" asked Linda.

"No thanks, I'm full of possum."

"Leave room for a huhu grub," said Angela.

"What's a huhu grub?"

"I'll eat one if you do, city boy. Follow me."

Angela led me to a tent on the other side of the field. A queue waited, and I craned my neck to see what they were eating.

I overheard two girls discuss the experience as they walked away.

"Did you swallow it whole?"

"Yep. You?"

"I just bit some off."

"What did it taste like to you? Peanut butter?"

"Yes! Peanut butter. Exactly what it reminded me of."

Angela grinned at me. "Are you ready for this?"

I rubbed my arms and looked around. My tummy felt like I was waiting in the queue for the school nurse's annual injection.

A large bowl contained a conglomeration of wriggling, white worm-like larvae, each the same size as a cocktail sausage but significantly more lively.

I frowned and recoiled.

"Are those the huhu grubs?" I asked.

"Yep," said Angela. "Yum."

"Yum? We're about to eat a living animal, and you say 'yum'? What are they? How do you eat them?"

Angela pointed to the other end of the table, where a customer handed over a bank note.

"They're a beetle larva. They cook them and give them to you on a stick."

"Seriously? Beetle larva? At least they're cooked, I suppose."

We shuffled forward and reached the front of the queue.

"How many?" asked the vendor, waving a spatula.

"Two please," I said. "Two, erm, huhu grubs."

The man offered me the two worms on sticks, as naturally as if he'd been serving cubed Cheddar and pineapple at a 1970s cocktail party.

"Four dollars please."

We took our spiked grubs and joined Fiona and Linda.

133

Angela waggled hers at me.

"Look, it's still alive."

I flinched and stepped backward. The three of them laughed.

"Want to try some, Fiona?" I asked.

I held up the grub to her face.

"Yuk," she said. "No thanks."

Angela gripped her stick and raised her eyebrows. "You first, city boy."

I put the grub up to my lips, opened my mouth, and pulled it away.

I looked at Angela. She smiled and nodded.

I inspected the huhu grub again, shut my eyes, and slid it on my tongue.

18. NOT LOOPIES

I closed my mouth, tugged the grub off the stick with my teeth, and bit.

It tasted of peanut butter.

I opened my eyes.

Angela chewed.

I swallowed.

"What did it taste like?" asked Fiona.

I gulped several times. "Peanut butter."

"You don't like peanut butter."

"I know. Can we find some water? I need a drink."

≈≈≈

Linda and Fiona assembled afternoon tea, while I perused the cartoons in the Christchurch news. The dunk-dunk-dunk of Frank's hammer echoed from the garden.

"Here's an idea," said Fiona. "Before I start work, why don't we take a tour around the South Island?"

She placed a plate of cakes in front of me. "Let's visit a few places you haven't seen and give Dad a chance to finish the hut. Just the two of us. We'll take the car and the tent."

"Sounds great," I said. "I love travelling with you. Where shall we go?"

"We could cross the pass, travel down the South Island, traverse the mountains again, and return via the glaciers."

"Are we going to be loopies?"

"We can't be loopies if we're locals."

"Am I a local?"

Fiona looked sideways at me.

"You're getting there."

I smiled, took a slurp of tea, and helped myself to one of Linda's home-made, square, sweet slices.

Fiona opened a road atlas and showed me a map of the South Island. She traced her finger across the page. "We could have a night in Christchurch, a couple of nights in Queenstown, a night at the glaciers, and then come home."

"Sounds great," I said. "But are we visiting anywhere you haven't seen before?"

"I've been to Queenstown. And the glaciers. And Christchurch, of course."

"Why don't we expand the trip?" I asked. "Let's visit places new to both of us?"

"Okay, but don't forget I start work at the hardware shop next Monday. We must be back before then. And remember our budget. We can spend what's in the bank; no more."

I opened the guidebook and scanned a section entitled *South Island Must-Sees.*

"How about this?" I said. "On the way to Queenstown, we could spend a night at Mount Cook Village and camp at the base of the Alps. Have you ever been there?"

"Nope," said Fiona.

"After Mount Cook, we can visit Oamaru. The guidebook says you can see wild penguins, and I've only ever seen a penguin in a zoo. Have you been to Oamaru?"

"I've been through Oamaru."

"But you didn't stop to see the penguins?"

"I think Dad was worried he'd be late for a horse race, so we didn't. I'm not sure we realized there were penguins."

"It's amazing how we see other countries before we experience our own, isn't it?" I said. "I know you've visited more of Britain than I have. Anyway, past Oamaru there's the city of Dunedin. Have you been there?"

Fiona narrowed her eyes. "Of course I've been there. My cousins live there."

"Right, but did you drive up the steepest street in the world?"

Fiona admitted this particular attraction had never featured on her radar.

"After Dunedin we can head down to Invercargill."

"Far out, Simon. What on earth is there to see in Invercargill? It's a cold, wet, and windy little town at the end of the world."

"You don't appreciate it if people say that about Hokitika."

"Come on, then. What does your guidebook list as the top attraction in Invercargill?"

"There's the airport."

"How exciting," said Fiona. "What's special about the airport?"

"It's where the flights take off to Stewart Island. The guide says Stewart Island is remote, untouched, and it's our best chance of encountering a wild kiwi bird."

I lay the guidebook on the table.

"We have to go there. I need to see a kiwi."

"Oh, right, kiwi birds. Sounds good. What's next, tour leader?"

I covered a smile with my hand and turned the page.

"After we return from finding kiwis, we can spend a day or two in Queenstown. It's the adventure capital of New Zealand."

"I know. I've been there."

"Did you do the white-water rafting, or the jet boat ride, or the bungy jumping?"

"I think we sat in a hotel, ate chips, and waited for Dad's race meeting to end."

"Exactly. We can have some excitement this time. Okay, have you been to Milford Sound? The guide describes it as the eighth wonder of the world."

"I haven't been there, but we're running out of days, aren't we? I think Milford takes hours to travel to."

"Let me look. Hmm, it's about six hours' drive from Queenstown. We'd need two days."

"We'll have to leave Milford for another time."

"That's a shame. All right, on our last night we can stop at Franz Josef Glacier."

"I've been there," said Fiona. "I climbed the glacier on a school trip."

I gazed into the distance. "I'd love to experience walking on a glacier. I studied glaciers in geography class, but I've never seen one."

I closed the guide and squeezed her shoulder. "This is so exciting, travelling by ourselves again."

Frank opened the kitchen door and stood on the step. He kicked his boots off.

"Brush off all that sawdust before you come in," said Linda. "It'll go everywhere."

137

The kitchen door closed, and we heard clothes being patted. Linda opened it.

"Not on the bloody step. Sweep it up."

We heard brushing. The door opened again. Frank entered, and a few wood shavings settled on the carpet. I covered them with my foot and hoped Linda hadn't noticed.

Phillip popped his head in.

"Tea, Phillip?" asked Linda. "And cake?"

"Cake? All right, I'll have a quick one before milking."

He pulled off his boots and joined us.

"We're going on a trip next week," said Fiona. "We're travelling around the South Island to show Simon some more New Zealand scenery."

Frank waved his arm in the direction of the mountains.

"Why would you want to go anywhere else," he asked, "when you've all this scenery here?"

Fiona ignored him.

"We're planning on seeing Mount Cook, Dunedin, and Queenstown," she said. "We're even hoping to reach Stewart Island."

"There are good racetracks in Dunedin and Queenstown," said Frank. He opened the newspaper. "I'll see if there are any races running while you're there."

"I'd love to visit Stewart Island," said Linda. "I've heard it's a beautiful place for tramping."

"You and your tramping," said Frank. "There's bush on the farm you could tramp in. No need for all these expeditions into uncharted territory."

"Frank doesn't understand the pleasure of getting lost in the woods," said Linda.

Frank finished his tea. "I'd better return to my carpentry. You'll want the hut ready for your homecoming." He departed via the kitchen door, leaving sawdust on the back of the chair.

Phillip stuffed a cake in his mouth and stood up. "No rest for the wicked, Simon. D'you want to fetch the cows? I'll start the milking machine."

≈≈≈

I sat at the dining table. Linda deposited steaming plates and pulled out a chair.

"Fish pie for dinner tonight, for a change. When are you two off?"

"Tomorrow morning," said Fiona.

"After milking?" I asked.

"All right," said Fiona. "After milking. I know how you enjoy it."

"It's a long way to drive from here to Mount Cook in one day," said Linda. "You could stay with Debbie on the way."

"She's been so good to us," said Fiona. "I don't want to impose on her, if we can avoid it."

I heard Phillip's motorbike pull up outside.

That's odd, he stays at his own house after evening milking. Is everything all right?

The kitchen door opened, and Phillip poked his head in.

"Are you confident at taking those cups off the cows, Simon?"

My fork paused halfway to my mouth.

"I think so. Why?"

"You remember I told you about my friend with the big rotary shed? The one where the cows ride around on a turntable?"

"Yes, I want to see that," I said.

"I spoke to him on the phone, and he needs a relief milker tomorrow night, but his usual chap's hurt his arm. I mentioned you were heading over the mountains, and he wondered if you could help?"

"Wow. I'd love to. But d'you think I'm good enough, Phillip? I haven't milked many times. And he knows I can only take the cups off, right? I can't run the milking all by myself or anything."

Phillip laughed. "You won't have to run the milking. He just wants someone to help. Oh, and he said they pay thirty dollars a shift. Is that enough for you?"

Enough? I'd do it for free.

"Hmm, I'm not sure." I turned to Linda. "Linda, what's the going rate for relief milking?"

She rolled her eyes and exhaled.

I grinned.

"Of course it'll be enough," I said. "So long as they don't expect a seasoned professional."

"Great. I'll tell him he's borrowing my farm worker. He said you could stay the night as well."

"Fantastic," said Fiona. "That's our first night's accommodation sorted."

South Island Tour

Fiona swung the Honda away from the crashing Tasman Sea breakers and accelerated towards the mountain passes.

Scenicland FM's signal faded into a crackle, and she turned the car radio off.

I wondered who'd remove the cows' cups at milking tonight.

I wondered who Angela would make fun of at dinner.

I wondered whether Jazz would miss riding on the four-wheel bike with me.

The West Coast had become my home, and although I didn't think the locals would ever consider me to be a native Coaster, people recognized me, even accepted me. My foreign novelty had begun to wear off.

The road to Christchurch curved into the foothills, and I studied the thick vegetation pouring down both sides. A grey scar betrayed a steep section where the land had slipped away and felled long, straight tree trunks, as if a giant had spilt a box of Swan Vesta matches.

Orange rotating lights approached on the roof of a white pickup truck. The driver flashed his headlights three times. Fiona removed her foot from the accelerator, and our car slowed with the uphill momentum.

The truck flashed its lights again.

"What does he want?" I asked.

"Not sure. Let's ask him."

The driver held a small, black walkie-talkie and gesticulated out of the window with his arm. The antenna twanged backward and forward.

We passed at walking speed.

The driver stabbed his radio's aerial towards the verge.

"Get off the road!" he said. "Get off the road!"

19. THE BOVINE ROUNDABOUT

Fiona slid onto the verge and applied the handbrake. I looked over my right shoulder and watched the truck's orange lights proceed down the road. A campervan parked on the grass behind us. The driver shrugged and lifted both arms with his palms upturned. He conversed with a lady in the front seat.

We waited.

Through the bushes framing the curved road ahead of us, I glimpsed more orange flashing lights.

Fiona drummed her fingers on the steering wheel.

"It'll be a wide load," she said.

I grabbed my camera and opened the passenger door.

The wonderful mountain smell of wet earth and lush greenery filled my nostrils. A Kea keeee-arrrd in the distance, and I smiled at my ability to associate the sound with an image of the bird.

Two more vehicles stopped behind the campervan.

"Look," called Fiona, from inside the car. "You won't have seen anything like this in England."

A yellow-and-black diagonally-striped sign mounted on a second pickup announced 'Convoy ahead'. I watched the grey-bearded driver give Fiona a thumbs up. He wound down his window and addressed the campervan driver. The camper manoeuvred further on to the verge, and I heard bushes scratch along the side of the vehicle.

A truck followed the second pickup. It occupied both lanes and some of the verge. Like a snail designed by Pablo Picasso, it carried a rectangular house on its back.

I stared.

It wasn't a house.

It was half a house.

The Māori driver steered with his left hand and addressed a walkie talkie with his right. He turned and offered us a wide, gap-tooth grin from his round face, under his beanie hat.

Someone had chopped the home in half before the residents had finished moving out. I stood on my tiptoes and observed carpets lining the floor, their frayed edges showing where the saw had bisected the dwelling. Faded curtains flapped, and an internal door swung and banged. I wondered if the fitted wardrobes still contained the occupants' clothes.

The house passed, and I shook my head. A final pickup followed, displaying a 'wide load ahead' sign on its rear. Two campervans and a saloon car pursued it, their drivers peering around the house to assess if they could overtake.

Fiona grinned and started the engine.

≈≈≈

"This," said John Parsons, "is our 44-stall rotary milking shed."

He ducked through an entrance and clumped into a large, metal, windowless building.

Shallow puddles glistened where the floor wasn't level. An industrial metal-platformed turntable occupied the centre of the space, and a complicated array of black hoses dangled down from overhead pipes. John unhooked a dark-green apron from a peg and handed it to me.

I opened my eyes wide. "This is incredible, being able to milk 44 cows at once."

John removed his cap and rubbed his bald head.

"We couldn't operate on this scale without a rotary shed," he said. "The cows walk in, step on the platform, we put the cups on, and they begin their fairground ride. Once they've completed one rotation, we remove the cups, they step off, and they head back to pasture. Well, most of them do. Number 873 likes to ride around again if she's allowed."

"Eight hundred and seventy-three? How many d'you milk here?"

"Just over fifteen hundred."

"Gosh. We milk two hundred on Frank's farm."

John chuckled. "I remember those little farms on the West Coast with their herringbone sheds. Anyway, this is where you'll be working."

He indicated a concrete trench, where a large plastic bottle stood filled with ochre liquid.

"D'you want me to spray as well?"

"Yes, please. Take the cups off, hang them up, and spray."

I closed my eyes and took a calming breath.

My first paid farm work. I'd better not stuff this up.

"Put the apron on, Simon," said John. "They'll be here in a minute."

He flicked a switch on the wall, and I heard the deep hum of his milking machine. I hooked the apron over my Massey Ferguson jumper. The cows' hooves clattered like a pantomime horse's tap-dance routine, as they entered along a metal walkway bordered by tubular rails and stepped onto the turntable. John attached the cups to each one. The cows began their circular journey as the milking platform rotated.

I watched the empty stalls approach and wondered how long it would be before the first udder required my attention.

The rear end of my initial customer approached.

I flipped off the milking cups and hung them up. An automatic jet rinsed the machine. I sprayed her a split-second before the next cow arrived. John didn't watch me and showed no interest in my activities.

Cups off, hang up, spray.

Cups off, hang up, spray.

Cups off, hang up, spray.

I lost count of the cows. I'd no idea how anyone could perform this activity every day, morning and evening. It wasn't the same as Frank's herringbone shed, where Phillip and I could have a chat, or listen to Scenicland FM, while the machine milked 24 stationary cows. My forearms and shoulders ached with the relentless, repetitive movement. Like a terrifying scene from a black-and-white Hitchcock movie, the cows never stopped coming.

Two hours later, John switched the machine off, and my ears accustomed to the quiet.

"Thanks, Simon," he said. "Are you okay to milk tomorrow morning as well?"

I removed my apron.

"Um, of course."

"Great, see you at four."

"Err, four? We don't start until six on Frank's farm."

≈≈≈

Fiona drove away from John's farm.

I slept.

I'd milked endless cows.

Twice.

The 3:30 alarm had beeped in the middle of a nightmare, where I dreamt I'd overslept, sprinted to the shed, and found the roundabout rotating at full speed, with a pile of cows sprawling over the floor, and milk squirting everywhere.

Muscles ached that I didn't know I owned. This wasn't the best start to our holiday, but at least I'd earned sixty dollars for the two shifts.

Fiona tapped my leg. "Wake up, you've slept for over two hours. You're missing the good bits. We'll arrive at The Church of the Good Shepherd soon."

I frowned, turned over in the passenger seat, and rested my head against the window. "What's so special about The Church of the Good Shepherd? I've seen hundreds of churches."

"This church is rather unique."

Fiona bumped into a gravel car park, and I braced myself on the dashboard. I stepped out, stretched, and felt immediate arm pain which reminded me of my morning's activities.

A solitary, granite building stood at the head of a lake.

I felt cool air on my cheeks and stared at the ice-blue water. If British Paint's marketing team had been here, they'd have frantically scribbled notes for their next colour-chart working group.

I breathed in the chill, put my hands on my hips, and gazed around the shores where the opaque turquoise water met the pine-tree green of the land. I wouldn't have been surprised to see a kilted piper step out from behind a tree and play 'Amazing Grace'.

"The lake doesn't look real," I said. "I've never seen a body of water so blue, so milky-aqua."

"Glacier water," said Fiona. "Wait until you see inside."

We mounted the three steps into the church. Fiona shivered as we entered the dim, stone building. Light shone from a window at the end of the nave.

Silence.

We paused at the entrance.

I reached for Fiona's hand and felt my mouth fall open.

Behind the altar of this church, something was missing.

20. THE CLOUD PIERCER

My jaw dropped, as I realised this church would never need stained glass. God himself had provided the design.

A simple cross stood on a stone ledge, silhouetted against a panoramic view of snow-capped mountains behind the tree-lined lake, visible through a transparent, rectangular, glazed opening.

No-one could build a church with a more awe-inspiring vista. If anything could persuade non-believers to begin their Christian journey, this view would be it.

Fiona squeezed my hand.

I realised I hadn't blinked.

The last time I'd seen an image this stunning was in a glossy, hardback book on a coffee table.

We drank in the chapel's peace and gazed in awe and wonder.

I tensed, as I heard a large diesel engine enter the gravel car park, and the scrunch of tyres.

We savoured our last minute of solitary contemplation.

The view.

The lake.

The mountains.

The sanctity.

A lady with coiffured hair and extravagant make-up appeared in the chapel's entrance. She grasped a walking stick in one hand and held on to the door frame with the other.

"Come on, Tyrus," she said, "the driver told us we had ten minutes."

A grey-haired, plump man followed her. He negotiated the three steps into the church with difficulty and paused at the top.

"Huh," said Tyrus. "Will ya take a look at that?"

A gaggle of elderly ladies waited behind him. They fanned past and brandished cameras. Tyrus stood in the doorway, leant on the wall, and puffed.

"Are you okay, honey?" said one of the ladies.

Another took his arm, and they shuffled down the aisle towards us.

In a harem of American pensioners, Tyrus represented the entire male population.

I couldn't decide if he was the luckiest octogenarian alive, or the unluckiest.

The ladies took turns at posing for photos with Tyrus in front of the altar.

One helped him pull his camera from a bag around his neck.

He seemed to enjoy his silverback status.

Fiona and I nodded a greeting, squeezed past them, and climbed back into the car.

≈≈≈

The Church of the Good Shepherd disappeared in our rear view.

We hurtled around country bends, the jagged line-graph of the Alpine peaks filling the windscreen at every turn.

I held on to the handle above the passenger door and braced myself for the tight corners.

"Fiona, stop."

"Here? Now?"

"Look." I pointed, as she pulled into a layby.

"What am I supposed to be looking at?" asked Fiona. She peered out of the window.

"Can't you see them?" I asked.

"I don't know what you're talking about."

"Sheep. Hundreds and hundreds of sheep."

"Yep, sheep. Why have we stopped for sheep?"

"It's what New Zealand's world-famous for. Everyone knows that."

"It is? Well, now you've seen some sheep."

I took a photo of the flock. Fiona spun the wheels and rejoined the road. She shook her head at me.

We rounded a corner, and I gasped at another impossibly aqua lake, a giant, opaque milky-blue swimming pool of colour. I raised my camera and lowered it again. I knew no matter how good a photo I took, I could never recreate this scenery.

"Lake Pukaki," said Fiona. "Also fed by glacier water."

"How can one country have so much stunning scenery? It doesn't seem fair. We have to take some photos. Nobody back in England will ever believe these views."

We pulled into an empty car park.

Enormous boulders lay around the edge.

Fiona opened the car boot.

"D'you want some lunch?" she asked. "I've brought crackers, cheese, and a couple of apples."

"I must take some photos. Before this… disappears."

"It won't disappear; the lake's been here thousands of years."

"It doesn't look real, the blue. It's like a David Hockney painting."

I placed the camera on top of a boulder.

"Shall we pose in the photo?"

"How?"

I pointed at a flat section of pebbles.

"If you stand by the round boulder, I'll set the self-timer. I'll leave the camera on this rock and run over to you."

"You want me to stand where?"

"On those pebbles. By the boulders."

"Um, okay."

Fiona scrambled over the rocks. She stood and put her hands on her hips. I bent down and spied her through the viewfinder.

"Not those pebbles." I pointed again. "The ones beside the round boulder."

"They're all round."

"That one." I jabbed my finger. "The round boulder near the lake."

Fiona stepped over two more rocks and turned to the camera.

"Ready?" I shouted.

"Yep," said Fiona, from the lakeside.

"Okay, smile."

I pressed the button. The camera beeped rhythmically.

I had ten seconds to stand next to Fiona, with my arm around her, in a photo we could develop in supersize, and hang on the wall of a future family home.

"Hurry up," she said.

I vaulted over the rocks, stood beside Fiona, and smiled at the camera.

"Did it take?" I asked her.

"No idea. I didn't see a flash or anything. The red light stopped blinking before you arrived."

"Damn. I don't think I was in the picture. I'll get another one to be certain."

I clambered back to the camera and inspected her through the lens again.

Both Fiona and the view continued to look equally stunning.

"Ready?"

"Still ready. Getting bored."

Beep…beep…beep…

I jumped on top of the first boulder, slipped, and threw my hands out to prevent myself from falling on my face.

I pushed myself up and heard the camera click behind me.

Clearly, a close-up of my bottom with Fiona and the lake in the background would not be an appropriate dinner-party conversation piece.

"You're never going to reach me in time," said Fiona. "Take a picture of the lake. We don't need to be in it."

≈≈≈

We continued our journey. At every bend, a fresh vista of the tree-lined water, fringed by low hills with the backdrop of the imposing mountains, formed another living-room-wall-worthy canvas. I leant out of the passenger window and held my camera.

The hairs on my bare forearm stood up.

"Did you feel that? The temperature dropped a few degrees."

"We're nearing the foothills. I'll need to put a jumper on."

Fiona stopped the car and dug warm clothes out of the boot. I opened my door, stared at the lake, took two more hopeless photos, and breathed in deep, clear, precious, mountain air.

Air that tasted primeval, unsullied by human activities.

The tour bus passed, leaving the smell of diesel as it disappeared around the next corner. My mouth turned down, and I sighed.

Brown grass lined a U-shaped valley floor with grey, gravel, river tentacles reaching across it. A perfect, play-school, triangular hill fronted higher peaks, the sun hanging above their summits. We crossed one-lane bridges, accelerated, and caught up with the bus.

The road ended at an extensive building called The Hermitage Resort.

I gazed at the isolated hotel and recalled a film scene where Jack Nicholson chops through a door with an axe.

The bus disgorged its passengers, and the driver pulled suitcases out of side hatches. Hotel staff wheeled brass trolleys across the car park. I glimpsed Tyrus hobbling into reception, ladies with blue-rinsed hair attached to both arms.

"I don't think we can afford to stay here," I said. "Where's the campsite?"

Fiona ruffled the map.

"We must have passed the turning. It's about one kilometre back."

She swung the wheel, we left The Hermitage, and forked up a single-lane road leading into a steep-sided gorge.

A sign indicated we were heading up the Hooker Valley.

Deserted.

Bleak.

Desolate.

I shivered all over and experienced a terrible feeling we might never come back.

≈≈≈

Fiona stopped the car beside a small sign advertising White Horse Hill: Mount Cook Department of Conservation campsite.

"Is this where we're staying?" I asked.

"Yep. Pull the tent out."

"But there's no kitchen or toilets or anything. And there are no other campers. Are you sure this is the right place?"

Fiona opened her eyes wide. "Would you prefer to sleep at the hotel with the tour bus passengers?"

"Of course not." I shivered. "They might be warmer tonight, though."

"Come on, give me a hand."

We erected the tent, threw our sleeping bags into it, sat on a rock, and ate left-over crackers and cheese.

I watched the last sun illuminate the mountain tops. I stared at the tallest mountain and decided it must be Mount Cook. Its summit dissolved into a small soufflé of white cloud.

Fiona's teeth chattered.

"I'm so cold," she said. "I'm going to sleep in my clothes tonight."

"Me too. It's freezing."

We snuggled into our sleeping bags. I switched on a torch and pulled the travel guide out of a bag.

The Mount Cook National Park, it informed me, consisted almost entirely of permanent snow and glacial ice. 22 of New Zealand's highest mountains stood within the park's boundaries including Mount Cook itself, the highest peak in New Zealand and Australia. Many famous climbers had ascended it; Edmund Hillary himself trained for Everest on Mount Cook's slopes.

Mountaineers, the guide continued, considered Mount Cook to be an advanced climb. Its slopes had claimed over 160 lives, primarily those of poorly equipped climbers, who underestimated the skills needed to ascend. The weather could change abruptly, and frequent storms rose out of nowhere. Europeans named the peak after Captain James Cook, but Māori people called it *Aoraki*, which meant 'cloud piercer'.

A-o-ra-ki.

Cloud piercer.

Māori names are so evocative.

I heard the sound of heavy boots and the rustling of a waterproof jacket.

"What's that noise?" I whispered.

I lowered the guidebook.

"Someone's outside," said Fiona. "Who would be all the way out here at this time?"

21. TWIZZLE

I heard a man clear his throat outside the tent.

"Hello, anyone home?"

Fiona stared at me and jerked her head twice sideways towards the door.

I unzipped the tent and poked my nose out, to find a man wearing a dark-green fleece crouching in the twilight outside.

"Good evening," he said. "Are you camping tonight?"

I thought this should be obvious, given that we were in sleeping bags lying in a tent.

"Yep, two of us."

His long brown beard and straggly hair draped over his top, which advertised he worked for the Department of Conservation.

"It's three dollars each for the night, please."

He pulled a small, printed pad and a marker pen out of his pocket, scrawled a big '6' on the top sheet and tore it off.

I wriggled my hand in my pocket and found six dollars.

"Thanks." He dropped the money into a bag around his waist.

"You must be experienced campers to be staying up here tonight."

"We've done a fair bit," I said. "Why d'you say that?"

"Rather you than me," he said. "I'd peg out a few more guy ropes if I were you."

He paused and scanned the sky. "Could become blowy later."

He reversed out of the tent, and his boots clump-clump-clumped as he walked away.

Dusk.

Silent.

Not a breath of wind.

I discovered the spare guy ropes and pegs in plastic wrapping, sealed as the day we'd purchased them from the camping store.

"D'you think that chap forecast the weather correctly?" I asked Fiona. "It's completely motionless out here."

"He's a conservation department worker," she said. "I'd listen to him. I think it's the calm before the storm."

The tent pegs bent in the hard ground. I laid them flat on a rock, banged them straight, and pegged out every guy rope we owned.

A nearby shrub formed the most convenient gentleman's toilet, so I made use of it, then stood with my hands on my hips, craned my head backward, and stared up.

So many stars.

So many pinpricks of twinkling white light.

So many suns, millions of light years away.

The black, jagged outline of the mountains loomed over our insignificant tent.

I'm Edmund Hillary at Everest camp four. All my companions have turned back except for the loyal Sherpa Fiona. We've been waiting for three days for the weather to clear. Tomorrow morning, before dawn, we're going to strike for the summit. We'll be the first people to climb the great, untamed peak. The pinnacle of humanity's earthly achievements. Our pictures will be in newspapers across the world. For a while, nobody will be more famous.

"Simon, what are you doing? Come to bed. I need you to warm me up."

Sherpa Fiona's voice sounded from inside the tent.

I zipped up the flap, lay down beside her, and hugged her tightly through our sleeping bags.

We lay in silence.

"It's so quiet," whispered Fiona. "It's eerie, like the part before the scary scene in a horror movie."

"Thanks a lot. We're lying in a tent, miles from civilization, and now I'm thinking about werewolves."

FLAP FLAP FLAP FLAP FLAP FLAP FLAP

"What's that?" asked Fiona.

We lay holding each other.

FLAP FLAP FLAP FLAP FLAP FLAP FLAP

"It's the tent. The wind's started. Now it's calm again."

"I'm not sure if I'll sleep tonight," said Fiona. "I'm so cold."

155

FLAP FLAP FLAP FLAP FLAP

FLAP

FLAP

"If this is what the conservation guy meant by a wind," I said, "I think we'll manage. He must have thought we were complete novices."

I hugged her tighter.

We lay still.

A rushing, whooshing began in the distance. I lifted my head. It sounded like someone had switched on a colossal, high-powered leaf-blower several kilometres away.

I let go of Fiona and knelt up.

"Which direction is that coming from?" I asked.

I couldn't see the tent entrance. I groped around for the torch and realised I couldn't illuminate wind.

The whooshing noise approached, faster and faster, louder and louder.

Fiona held my shoulder.

"Simon, I'm scared."

FLAPFLAPFLAPFLAPFLAPFLAPFLAPFLAP

I clapped my hands over my ears.

Fiona grabbed my arm and pulled me down against her.

The tent flattened. Its roof touched my head.

FLAPFLAPFLAPFLAPFLAPFLAPFLAPFLAP

We gripped each other. I gritted my teeth and clenched my eyes shut.

The squall passed.

Silence.

"What the hell was that?" I asked.

"Wind," said Fiona.

"Thank you, Captain Obvious. I've never experienced wind like that in my life."

I unzipped the tent.

Fiona pulled my hand. "Stay here with me."

"I'm not going far; I want to see what happened."

The stars shone as peacefully as in a tranquil nativity scene on a Victorian Christmas card. The distinct, black outline of the mountains continued to dominate the background.

"I'm still cold." Fiona reminded me of my obligation to be a human radiator.

I lay down with her again.

She drifted to sleep in my arms.

Sleep.

The three-quarter sleep before you succumb to unconsciousness.

The part where you have half-dreams.

The part where you wonder if they're real or imagined.

In the distance the giant leaf-blower restarted.

Fiona snuggled against me.

"I'm glad we're lying in the tent," she whispered. "If our weight wasn't holding it down, it would blow away."

The wind blasted like an inter-city train flying through a minor station.

We held on tight.

FLAPFLAPFLAPFLAPFLAPFLAPFLAPFLAPFLAP

The tent flattened again.

The roof squashed against my shoulder.

FLAPFLAPFLAPFLAPFLAPFLAPFLAPFLAPFLAP

I heard a guy rope ping outside. And a second one.

Calm.

I clicked on the torch and opened the tent door.

"Where are you going?" said Fiona. "Stay here."

"I'm pegging the guy ropes back in. They pinged out."

"Leave them. You'll be banging them in all night. Come and keep me warm, for goodness' sake. Stop letting all the heat out."

I zipped up the flap and lay down next to her.

I kissed her forehead.

"Where's the wind coming from?" asked Fiona.

"I think it's whooshing down the mountains. This campsite's at the foot of the Hooker glacier, and the wind's rushing down the face. There's a name for that type of wind. It's on the tip of my tongue. Phonetic wind? Frenetic wind? I learnt it in geography. Hang on."

I put my hand on my chin and shut my eyes.

I opened them and held up one pointed finger.

"Katabatic. That's it. Katabatic wind. Wind carrying heavy air down a slope by gravity."

"I wish it would stop carrying it," said Fiona. "We'll never have any sleep."

FLAPFLAPFLAPFLAPFLAPFLAPFLAPFLAP

The katabatic squalls continued.

Fiona slept.

I lay awake. One of us needed to keep watch.

Dawn.

I distinguished the outline of the tent entrance.

The fabric rustled.

Fiona turned over in her sleep.

I hoped she wouldn't mind driving; my eyes hadn't closed the whole night.

I wriggled out of my sleeping bag, unzipped the tent, shuffled forward, and stood up.

The mountain tops hid in flocks of grey clouds, herded by the sheepdog of a brisk breeze.

I stretched, walked a few steps, and watered my favourite bush.

Fiona woke when I crinkled a cereal packet. She rubbed her eyes and blinked at me.

"We're still alive, then."

"What's the time?" I asked.

Fiona patted the tent floor and discovered her watch. "Seven o'clock. I think I slept. I'm not sure. The wind; I've never heard anything like it."

"Mmm, I'm not sure I want to hear it again. Can you drive? I haven't slept at all. How far are we travelling today?"

Fiona pulled out the road atlas and handed it to me.

I yawned and covered my mouth.

My finger traced across the map.

"Mount Cook Village has one road in and out," I said, "so we'll follow the edge of the lake again."

"I don't mind," said Fiona. "I'll never tire of that view."

"After the lake, we'll turn right and head through somewhere called Twizzle."

Fiona laughed. "It's called Twizel. Twy-zel. Not Twizzle."

"Right. Twy-zel. Then we make a left turn at a place called Omarama."

I pronounced it to rhyme with 'panorama'.

Fiona giggled. "O-mah-rah-maah. Not O-maah-raah-mah."

"And after O-mah-rah-maah we head down to the coast to Oamaru, where we might see the wild penguins."

"At least you pronounced Oamaru correctly."

I rummaged in the bag. "Let's eat breakfast and get going. Oh. We didn't bring any milk. D'you want dry Nutrigrain, or d'you want to pick up something in Twizzle?"

Fiona poked me.

"Let's buy something in Twizzle, as you call it. I expect you need a coffee."

"I'll need about three, if I'm going to have any chance of staying awake."

We packed up the tent. I discovered five pegs several metres away, tossed like miniature Olympic javelins by the katabatic wind.

In the straight, U-shaped valley we overtook the tour bus.

"I wonder where they're going today."

"Probably to Queenstown."

"They're missing the best parts; we're not. I think the South Island deserves more time. D'you think the wind kept them awake?"

≈≈≈

The manager of the Twizel bakery raised her head, as I crashed open her glass door and rubbed my face. I held the entrance for Fiona and surveyed the store.

"A strong coffee, please, and a hot chocolate. D'you sell any breakfast-type food?"

"I have bread and cakes. I could make you a sandwich?"

"Which flavour sandwich fillings d'you have, please?"

"Ham or Cheese."

This wasn't exactly Prêt à Manger.

"Can you toast them?"

"Yep, fifty cents extra."

"Go halves?" said Fiona.

"One toasted ham and one toasted cheese sandwich, please. And the coffee, and hot chocolate."

We sat at a corner table, ate the sandwiches, and slurped the hot drinks. The coffee gave me an artificial awake feeling.

Fiona drove.

We turned left in O-mah-rah-maah and replaced cloudy mountain peaks with low hills bordered by sporadic glimpses of a wide, gravel riverbed.

An occasional farm truck passed.

My head nodded.

I jerked my neck back and forced my eyes open with my thumb and forefinger.

I stared at the brown, denuded hillsides.

Rain spattered on the windscreen.

Fiona switched on the wipers.

I watched them swish left to right.

I closed my eyes.

Fiona jammed her foot on the brake, swerved off the road, and skidded on the gravel verge.

I rubbed my forehead. "Ow, why d'you do that?"

She pointed. "Look. Coming towards us."

22. 1980s PUNK EYE SHADOW

A campervan approached. The driver and passenger waved and grinned. Something was very wrong with the scene.

I frowned, glanced at Fiona, and watched them pass.

Fiona gesticulated at them.

It took me a few seconds to work out what had caused her to skid off the road.

"Woah, they were driving on the wrong side. It's lucky you noticed. I hope they realise their mistake, before they kill anyone."

"It's common in remote areas," said Fiona. "Tourists from overseas forget we drive on the left in New Zealand. They pull out of a campsite or a lunchtime picnic spot, they see no other cars, and they head off on the right-hand side. Sometimes they travel for miles before they realise."

She engaged gear and pulled away from the verge.

Rows of poplars sheltered occasional farmhouses. I frowned and shook my head at a row of pylons, marching across the top of the Beatrix Potter lakeside hills like extras from War of the Worlds.

Fiona slowed down, as we entered small towns straddling our route.

"Speed cameras," she said. "Just the place to encounter a bored country cop."

At the phenomenally Scottish-sounding settlement of Duntroon we found one.

The officer stood outside a café. He leant against his chessboard-marked saloon car, sipped from a paper cup, and read a newspaper spread across the bonnet.

"Fiona, can we stop here please? I need another coffee. I'm struggling to stay awake. This place looks like it sells take-aways."

Fiona parked opposite the police cruiser.

"D'you want anything?" I asked her.

"No thanks, I'll stay in the car."

The policeman scrutinized me, as I stretched and yawned. He wore a light-blue, short-sleeved shirt, a peaked cap, and a dark vest with his radio attached to it.

I nodded at him as I crossed the road.

"Have you come far today?" he asked.

His shirt tucked into his trousers roughly, and his flotation-ring tummy precipitated over his belt, suggesting he spent much of his life immobile in his car.

"We've driven from Mount Cook. We were camping there."

"Blowy last night, was it?"

"I hardly slept."

"It's a good job your young lady's driving. We wouldn't want you to nod off at the wheel."

I thought of something I should tell him.

"I saw a campervan earlier. They were on the wrong side of the road."

"I've already spoken to one lot this morning. Might be the same ones. Bloody loopies."

"Yep," I agreed. "Bloody loopies."

"I'd better carry on," said the cop. "Drive carefully." He winked. "And make sure you stay on the left."

He folded his newspaper, placed his empty cup in a rubbish bin, and opened his car door.

I stepped into the shop and ordered a coffee.

The lady behind the counter smiled.

"Morning. What did Geoff have to say?"

"Geoff?"

"The policeman."

"Oh, we were talking about loopies driving on the wrong side of the road."

"There's a lot of that," she said. "And camping where they're not supposed to, leaving rubbish by the lakes. Unfortunately, we need their business."

She handed me the coffee. I paid her, crossed the road, and slumped back into the passenger seat. The coffee burnt my tongue, and I wedged it in the door pocket.

Fiona glanced at the police car. She poodled towards the town boundary at one kilometre per hour below the speed limit.

I squirmed to find a comfortable position.

≈≈≈

I woke when Fiona turned off the engine.

"Where are we? I must have fallen asleep."

"Penguin car park. Or at least I think it is. There's no-one here."

"I don't see any penguins."

"They won't be in the car park, silly. They'll be near the beach. Let's have a read of the information board over there."

I reached into the seat pocket for my coffee, sipped it, and choked.

"I need another drink. This one's cold."

"Okay, we'll find a café. After we've seen the penguins."

Native bushes fringing the car park rustled in the stiff breeze. A discarded pamphlet vortexed, then lodged in a tree branch. A sea-bird called. It soared sideways and disappeared into the sky.

I traced my finger over a map on the information board. A worn-out hole showed where multiple preceding visitors had done the same thing. Fiona studied the description.

"Penguin viewing: December to February," she said. "I suppose that's peak tourist season."

"It's March."

"I know it's March. We might not see them."

"Great. Can we buy that coffee?"

"At least let's stroll down to the beach. The map says it's a short but steep walk."

She pointed at a symbol of a stick-man careering down a near-vertical precipice.

The gravel scrunched behind us, and I turned to see a fit-looking older man. He wore the same Department of Conservation uniform as the employee who'd taken our camping money at Mount Cook. His tousled grey hair and ruddy face indicated the effects of outdoor employment.

"Hello, you two," he said, as if he knew us. "Have you come to see the penguins?"

He offered us a lopsided smile under his hook nose.

"Yes," said Fiona, "but it seems we're too late. It's March."

"Oh, I think we might find you a couple. I'm Stuart, the ranger here."

He offered me his hand to shake. It felt rough, like Frank's.

163

"We run tours in summer, as there are not enough visitors to warrant them at other times. Where are you guys from?"

"The West Coast," said Fiona. "Hokitika."

"I've got a farmer friend there," said Stuart.

Here we go. The South Island village.

Stuart continued, "D'you know a Frank Wall?"

"I'm his daughter, Fiona."

"Well. blow me down," said Stuart. "I haven't seen Frank for years. We used to meet at the horse racing, but he doesn't seem to come this way anymore. I still receive a Christmas card though."

He smiled, revealing crooked, yellow teeth.

"This is my partner, Simon," said Fiona, "from London."

"Are you enjoying New Zealand?" asked Stuart. "Bit different to London, I expect."

I agreed it was different to London.

"Anyway, penguins," said Stuart. "There are no organised tours in March, but I'll give you a private one." He winked. "As you're Frank's daughter. Follow me."

He strode to the edge of the car park. Fiona and I hurried after him.

"Most penguins spend their days out at sea," Stuart explained, turning his head over his shoulder and sweeping his arm, in a movement that encompassed the entire Southern Ocean. I strained my neck forward to hear him above the wind. "They fish all day and return at dusk when predators are less likely to see them. We've two types of penguins here. Little Blue penguins are the smallest in the world; they'll be at sea now. They're the ones the loopies come for."

"What's the other type?" asked Fiona, as she struggled to keep up with Stuart on the uneven, steep, downhill path.

"Yellow-eyed penguins. Up here."

Stuart deviated from the track, pushed aside two bushes, and stepped between them. He crouched down and pointed.

His voice dropped to a loud whisper.

"Here's a pair. They're nesting. We need to be quiet so's not to scare them."

We knelt alongside him. My knee connected with a jagged stone, and I winced and shouted *Ow* in my head.

Two small penguins sat under a scraggly bush. Their white tummies and black backs resembled birds I'd seen at London Zoo, but their soft, fluffy, brown heads intrigued me. Their long beaks culminated in a badly drawn, bright-orange, round tip. It reminded me of teenage girls in a nightclub who'd reapplied lipstick after too many Smirnoffs. A pastel band of yellow circled the penguins' eyes and extended around the sides of their heads like 1980s punk eye shadow.

"Wow," I whispered to Stuart. "These are the first wild penguins I've ever seen."

"The one on the right's the male," he said, quietly.

"I can't believe we're this close to them," said Fiona.

"I wouldn't normally bring anyone to their nests," said Stuart, "but they haven't seen people for a while, so it'll be okay."

"Is it all right to take a photo?" I asked him.

"Sure," said Stuart, "but please turn off your flash, and if you see penguins anywhere else, never stick your camera down their burrows. It blinds them."

The first male penguin I'd ever seen in the wild regarded me indignantly, like a plump aristocrat in a Mayfair gentlemen's club inspecting a junior member.

His mate shyly turned her head to one side. I raised my camera. The male appeared more disgusted, and I wondered if I should request his permission to photograph them. Rather rudely I took the picture anyway.

The male blinked at me and shuffled his feet.

"We'd better leave them," whispered Stuart.

I said a silent goodbye to the penguins.

The male regarded the insignificant humans and blinked again.

We reversed out of the clearing.

"Thanks, Stuart," I said, as soon as we were together on the track. "Wild penguins, gosh. I always imagined I'd have to visit the South Pole to see them."

"I have to go now," said Stuart, "but if you continue down the track to the beach, you'll come across New Zealand fur seals. Don't approach them. They're bigger than you, and I don't want to have to treat a seal bite."

"Thanks, Stuart," said Fiona, "I'm glad we met you."

"Give my regards to Frank." He waved and marched towards the car park.

The path continued down the steep cliff face. We glimpsed the grey sea through the penguin bushes.

I gazed down at the empty beach. The seals must have arranged an appointment elsewhere.

"There's nothing between here and Antarctica," said Fiona, as she held her hand to her eyes and stared across the ocean.

This hadn't occurred to me before.

We were nearly as far South as it was possible to be. On the entire planet.

I watched the horizon, but I couldn't see any icebergs.

"How far is it?" I asked Fiona.

"It's about a five-hour flight," she said. "I applied for a job there once."

"That's a long way to commute."

"Not every day, obviously. Six months on and six months off, supporting the scientists."

I put my arm around her. Fiona had such adventurous spirit. I'd never met anyone else who would consider living in Antarctica.

"Come on," she said. "Let's find these seals."

The bottom of a set of wooden steps plunged into a dune, and we jumped onto the beach. Fiona stood by the water's edge, staring up at the craggy cliffs.

I took her photo.

She didn't look in the lens.

She looked at something behind me.

23. JUMBO MALTESERS

I swivelled to discover what had attracted Fiona's attention, but I could only see the beach, the cliffs, and the piles of brown, leathery boulders at their base.

"Look." Fiona pointed.

One boulder moved.

It sat up and shuffled down the beach towards the water.

It paused and realized it had company.

I moved nearer to my girlfriend. I'd no idea how to protect her from a big, brown, shuffling boulder but it felt like the right thing to do.

The boulder-seal lifted its head, sniffed the air, and began an ungainly lollop towards the surf.

We watched, amazed it could move so fast.

It hesitated at the water's edge, ogled us briefly, and plunged into the waves. Its tail disappeared, and the surf rolled in, as if the seal had never existed.

"I reckon that was a young one," said Fiona. "The other seals look a lot bigger."

"Erm, we shouldn't walk any closer to them," I said, as a different boulder turned over in its sleep.

Fiona held my hand. "Come on, let's find that coffee."

Many years had passed since my childhood holidays in the Scottish Highlands, but I recognized Oamaru's heritage instantly.

Strong, stone buildings formed the main street, accompanied by a war memorial and an imposing clock tower. The grey eiderdown of cloud matched the colour of the architecture and assisted with the comparison.

"We could be in Inverness," I said.

"There's a Scottish influence in this part of New Zealand," said Fiona. "You might notice a difference in the accent, too. People roll their 'r's."

I paused outside a shop window, which displayed an array of square slices, laid out temptingly like jumbo cubes of Cadbury's Dairy Milk.

"Here's a bakery," I said. "They sell hot drinks. And those cakes look good too."

"I'll have a read of the guidebook while you grab your coffee," said Fiona.

"D'you want anything?"

"No, thanks, I'll wait for lunch."

I stood behind a queue in the bakery. A queue of one. Unfortunately, the bakery assistant knew the entire queue personally.

I overheard a detailed description of a mutual acquaintance's recent divorce.

The meeting's agenda ran through several points, in a prolonged discussion to assess which party could be held accountable for this separation.

I tapped my foot and cleared my throat, although I had a secret desire to discover whether Rod was such a bastard as we understood Julie had implied.

The conversation progressed to Any Other Business, and somebody's upcoming hen night. I tried to piece together whether the imminent nuptials were in any way connected to Rod and Julie's break-up, when a bell tinkled, and another lady entered.

The queue paused for breath and peered over her shoulder.

She appeared surprised the shop contained any other customers, announced to the assistant that they must catch up soon, picked up her purchases, and departed.

"Can I help you?" the short, rotund, rosy-cheeked bakery assistant asked, her mouth in a straight line.

Her hair net sat askew and didn't completely cover her curly fringe.

"Hello. A coffee, please, and what are those brown, square cakes?"

"They're caramel slices, the best ones in New Zealand."

I wondered if she'd personally sampled all of them to arrive at this conclusion.

"One, please. I love caramel slice."

She picked up a pair of tongs and slid the slice into a small, white paper bag.

"Seven dollars please."

I paid her, and the shop bell jingled as I departed.

"Wow, what have you bought?" asked Fiona.

"Coffee, and the best caramel slice in New Zealand, apparently."

"Yum. Can I have some?"

"I could go back to the shop and buy you another one?"

"But I don't want a whole one. I just want a bit of yours."

I made a mental note to include in any future marriage vows, "I promise faithfully to splice a chunk off every cake I ever buy."

"All right, I'll give you a morsel."

We sat on a bench, I sipped my coffee, and took a bite of the best caramel slice in New Zealand.

The plump lady's cake appraisal was entirely accurate. The chocolate top cracked satisfyingly, the gooey caramel extruded at the correct rate of elasticity, and my teeth struggled to close around the appropriately thick and buttery biscuit base.

"Can I have my bit?" asked Fiona. "I don't want much."

I passed her the paper bag, and she reached in and snapped off half the slice.

"Oops, sorry," she said. "I couldn't take any less. The topping's rather hard."

We shared the chocolate, caramel, and biscuit. I was relieved Fiona had no designs on my coffee.

"Ready to move on?" she asked, as she brushed crumbs from her face.

I considered returning to the bakery and buying another slice, but I didn't want to spoil lunch.

"Where's the next stop?" I asked. The windscreen wipers swished, as a light drizzle began.

"Moeraki boulders," she said. "It's a short drive. You'll never have seen anything like these."

≈≈≈

Fiona tugged the drawstrings of her hood, and we stepped around puddles in the Moeraki boulders' car park.

I glanced fondly at the lights which shone from the windows of the Boulder View café.

"These boulders better be worth it," I said. "I've seen more rain here than the so-called wet West Coast."

"Stop complaining. You're about to experience the New Zealand equivalent of Stonehenge."

"Where are they, then?" I asked. I hunched my back, shivered, and regretted wearing short trousers.

"This way." Fiona took my hand, and we braced ourselves against the weather.

The New Zealand equivalent of Stonehenge comprised a row of oversized, brown basketballs dumped in shallow water at the edge of the ocean. Surf broke over their shiny, outer coating as if a giant had spilt a bag of jumbo-sized Maltesers.

Fiona turned her back to the intermittent rain and flicked through the guidebook.

"These boulders," she said, "formed 65 million years ago. They weigh several tonnes each and are approximately two metres across."

I removed my shoes, splashed through the shallows up to a globe-shaped boulder, and placed my hand on it.

I surveyed the ocean.

I imagined the scene at the time these formations were created. No humans.

Large prehistoric animals, or dinosaurs.

"How did they arrive here?" I asked Fiona. "I mean, if they're 65 million years old, they're significantly older than Stonehenge. They pre-date Homo sapiens."

She read from the guidebook. "The Māori believe the boulders are gourds, lost overboard from a great voyaging canoe called Araiteuru, wrecked on these shores hundreds of years ago."

I tried to picture a vessel large and sturdy enough to hold these colossal, spherical rocks.

The drizzle intensified. Fiona stuffed the guidebook into her jacket pocket.

The boulders weren't going to do anything more exciting, so I splashed out of the water and took Fiona's hand.

"Shall we grab some lunch at that café?"

"Good idea."

A tour bus engine rattled to a stop. The bus disgorged a crowd of Nikon-wielding, raincoat-clad tourists.

"Let's order before this group," I said. "If we're queued behind them, we'll be waiting all afternoon."

We strode into the café. The board above the serving area advertised the succinct menu, with a single hot food option. A lady with a pen behind her ear leant on the counter.

"I guess we'll have two fish and chips," I said. "And a large coffee and a hot chocolate."

The lady wrote on a pad and indicated we should choose a seat.

The tour group entered, and the din of rapid conversation increased, in a language I didn't recognize. They shook out multiple umbrellas and hung coats on the back of chairs.

We selected a small table and waited.

I glanced towards the kitchen.

Culinary activity increased, and the two chefs laid out plates. They dropped a sneeze of salad onto each one. I heard a deep-fat fryer crackle.

A waitress brought out two servings.

"Here we go," I said to Fiona. I unfolded a paper napkin.

She walked past our table to the tour group and placed the dishes in front of them.

A second server followed her with another two portions of fish and chips.

My fingers tapped the table.

"That's not right," I said. "We placed our orders first."

"Perhaps they pre-ordered?" said Fiona.

The servers brought more plates, and the tour group began eating.

They finished one by one, stood up, collected their umbrellas from near the door, and departed.

We were once again the sole customers.

I approached the counter.

"Erm, is our food going to be long?"

"What food?" said the server. She wiped the bench and stacked paper serviettes.

"The order of two fish and chips."

She searched the serving area.

She picked up containers and inspected the counter under them.

She examined the floor around her feet.

"We don't have an order for two fish and chips. We must have lost it. We had a bus tour to deal with, you see."

I stared at her with my mouth open and my eyes wide.

Is this the first time you've received a visit from a bus tour? Aren't you attached to the Stonehenge of New Zealand?

"So can we have our fish and chips now?" I asked.

"Dave, any fish left?"

"Nah, all gone. The tour group ate the last of them."

She turned to me and folded her arms. She breathed out through thin lips.

"We could make you some chips by themselves. It'll take a while, though."

I exaggerated a sigh.

"Don't bother," I said. "We'll find somewhere else."

I picked up the car keys.

"They've run out of food. And they don't want our business. Let's go."

My tummy rumbled like the sound of the Westland Dairy milk tanker thundering down Frank's drive, as I dropped into the driver's seat.

Fiona slid in beside me. She shook out the map.

"Where's the next place to buy lunch?" I asked.

"Dunedin, I reckon. It's about twenty kilometres away."

The road curved inland at a place called Shag Point. Fiona found this amusing.

We passed a welcome sign at the entrance to the city.

"Dunedin," said Fiona, "means 'Edinburgh' in Scottish."

"I'm starving," I said. "I could eat a bloody haggis. First food place we see, I'm stopping."

After a few city blocks, we discovered a Kentucky Fried Chicken in all its international marvellousness and ordered two boxes of chicken and chips.

"What did you say you wanted to do in Dunedin?" asked Fiona, as she stuck her fingers in her mouth and pulled them through her lips.

"I want to drive up the steepest street in the world," I said. "Is there anything else?"

"Do we have to drive up it? Can't we just look? I don't want to hurt the car."

She slurped the bottom of a Coke through a straw and glanced left and right to see if any other diners had noticed the noise.

"The people who live there must ascend it every day," I said. "It'll be fine."

"Hmmm. Anything else?"

"I'm sure there are loads more sights to see in Dunedin, but we're staying the night in Invercargill, and that's still ninety minutes away."

≈≈≈

"Baldwin Street," read Fiona, "a short street of 350 metres long, was officially crowned the steepest street in the world by Guinness World Records in 1987. Its lower gradients are one-in-five, which is unexceptional, however near the summit it angles at one-in-three."

I ratcheted the handbrake and parked at the bottom.

"Wow, I've never heard the words 'street' and 'summit' used in the same sentence."

Fiona continued reading. "The top of the street needed to be laid in concrete, as the city engineers expected bitumen to flow downhill on hot days."

She folded the book in her lap.

"Can you believe that?" she said. "It's so steep, the road surface might run away."

I engaged first gear, pulled into the centre of the road, stopped, and took a deep breath.

Fiona shook her head, rolled her eyes, and stared out of the passenger window.

I gazed at the perpendicular scene in front of us.

I'd never seen a street with steps in the pavement. Young tourists walked up them, taking pictures. Some lay on the roadway while their friends photographed them. One girl stood in a resident's terraced front garden, as another lady snapped her.

I wondered if the local inhabitants felt annoyed at sightseers photographing their properties, puffing and panting outside as they climbed, or doing what we were about to do.

"It doesn't look steep from the car," said Fiona.

"Ready to do this?" I asked.

"All right, get it out of your system. Drive up the steepest street if you have to."

I revved the engine like Damon Hill at the starting grid of the Adelaide Grand Prix.

The tourists stopped taking pictures of gardens. Their cameras swung around to face us.

We weren't the first car to do this, and we weren't going to be the last.

I pushed the throttle again, to give the tourists something to talk about.

I'm a famous urban rally driver in an endurance test of the toughest city environments in the world. Fans are lining the streets; the Champagne's on ice waiting for me. I just have to complete this last hill, and I'm on the podium.

Fiona looked at her watch. "Stop playing with the engine and get on with it."

I released the handbrake and set off in first gear.

The spectators raised their cameras as we passed. One man with a reversed baseball-cap fist-pumped the air. I waved out of the window and grinned.

The tachometer red-lined as we approached the summit.

Fiona gripped her seat.

"Put her into second gear. The engine's going to overheat."

"I can't change out of first," I shouted, above the seven thousand RPM. "I can't lose momentum."

The engine screamed up the steepest part of the hill.

I realized the car would cross a junction at the top, and we'd have to give way to traffic.

"Simon!" shouted Fiona. "How are we going to stop?"

24. INSIDE OR OUTSIDE

The suspension bounced, and we flew over the crest of Baldwin Street like one of the more exciting scenes from *The Dukes of Hazzard*. I applied the handbrake and grinned at Fiona.

The entire experience had lasted less than thirty seconds.

Fiona's panting sounded like Jazz on the four-wheel bike. She glared at me.

"You were bloody lucky there weren't any cars coming."

I executed a three-point-turn, sat up, and peered forward over the lip of the street.

"So, this is what Eddie the Eagle feels like."

"Now what?" asked Fiona.

"Now we drive down again."

We began a sedate descent. I gripped the wheel, and my foot remained on the brake.

The air stank of burning brake pads.

Fiona took a photo of Baldwin Street from the bottom.

It didn't look as spectacular a gradient as our experience suggested.

The tourists turned around to see where the brake pad smell came from. One of them raised her camera.

I lifted both my arms in a victory stance.

The winner of the New Zealand Urban Driving Endurance Event took the podium.

I bowed left and right.

Fiona rolled her eyes.

We hunched our bodies into the wind as we walked up to the glass-fronted door of the Invercargill campground. The manager turned the key in the lock. She opened it again as we approached.

"I'm just closing up. Can I help you?"

"D'you have a tent site for tonight, please?"

"Inside or outside?"

"We're camping."

"Yep. Inside or outside?"

This was a concept I'd never considered before.

"What's the difference?"

I glanced out of the window. Leaves danced around in circles, and tree branches folded diagonally.

"You could pitch your tent outside, and take your chances with tonight's weather, or we have an old barn where you'll be sheltered."

"It is more expensive?"

"Seven dollars a night outside; eight dollars a night inside."

"I don't want another night like Mount Cook," I said to Fiona.

The reception door clattered and blew open. I leant on it and pushed it shut.

I turned back to the manager. "We'll take inside, thanks."

"How many nights?"

"One, please. We're headed to Stewart Island tomorrow."

"You are? My friend runs the backpackers' campsite there. Her brochure's here somewhere."

She fished under her desk and handed me a pamphlet, with a photo of a short, fluffy bird.

I showed the picture to Fiona and grinned.

"Are you crossing to the island by boat or by plane?" asked the manager.

"We were planning on travelling by boat, to save money."

"I'd recommend taking the plane, unless you have steel stomachs. It's more expensive, but far pleasanter."

"Thanks for the advice, but we haven't booked it."

"That won't matter. Turn up at the airport. The first flight leaves at 9.30 in the morning, but if the plane's full, they'll return, and pick up extras. In the tourist season, they shuttle back and forward all day. Anyway, that's eight dollars please. The barn's the building at the back of the field."

She pointed behind us.

I paid her eight dollars. Fiona opened the door, and it blew out of her hand.

We pulled our tent and backpack from the car and strolled across the field. A few brave campers sat outside their tents, eating dinner, or smoking cigarettes.

"They're saving a dollar," I said. One dollar isn't anything to pay for a good night's sleep."

We laid out the tent in the barn, and I experimented with sticking a peg through the soft straw. Hard mud underneath resisted my attempts.

"Don't bother," said Fiona. "There's no wind in here, thank goodness."

"Are you hungry?" I asked.

"I could eat something. Let's drive into town."

I peered left and right, as we cruised along Invercargill's main street.

"I don't want McDonald's," I said. "We ate Kentucky for lunch."

"How about Cobb and Co.?" said Fiona. She pointed at a sign.

"What's Cobb and Co.?"

"A family restaurant, like Harvester in England. Dad always took us there when we were kids."

Over roast chicken, chips, and gravy, we discussed our plans.

Fiona talked about the new job she was starting on Monday. We both knew it wasn't a career, but it would bring in some much-needed income.

I had no idea what I was going to do with myself.

My role as an unpaid farm worker contributed to our lives in Hokitika, but it could never be a sustainable existence.

I needed a future.

≈≈≈

I awoke the following morning, stepped out of the tent, and stretched. I peered up at the high, wooden beams of the barn roof and realised the last time I'd camped indoors was aged seven, under the dining-room table.

"Wake up, Fiona. We've got a plane to catch."

"I could sleep in here forever," she said. "So dark and peaceful."

We packed up and walked past the pancaked tents of campers who'd elected to stay outdoors.

"I've never been more happy to spend a dollar," I said.

"Poor people," said Fiona.

≈≈≈

Invercargill airport.

Wet.

Bleak.

Deserted.

Diagonal rain gusted across the empty asphalt and made me feel like we'd parked the car at the end of the world, which in many ways we had.

Fiona braced herself, pulled up her hood, and sprinted over to read the parking sign, then vanished into the airport building.

I sheltered in the passenger seat and pulled out the guidebook.

Stewart Island, it said, or *Rakiura* as the Māori knew it, was New Zealand's third largest island, yet it was almost uninhabited. The population of just 450 people congregated in a single town, while the rest of the island consisted of forest, hills, and beaches. Temperatures were mild, but the weather could change from brilliant sunshine to torrential rain, and back to sunshine, in a few minutes.

I glanced up and watched the deluge hammer on the windscreen.

Stewart Island locals, the guide continued, remained suspicious of outsiders, mainlanders, laws, and bureaucracy. Captain Cook was the first white man to sight the location, but he couldn't decide if it comprised an island or a peninsula, and he called it, unimaginatively, Cape South.

I ruminated on being a sailor aboard a small wooden ship, passing these shores in this constant gale.

Fiona returned and knocked on my window. I opened it a crack, and raindrops fell on my open book.

"D'you have two dollars for parking?" she asked.

179

I undid my seatbelt and felt in my pocket.

"Yep, but how long does two dollars buy us?"

"It's two dollars forever. You pay two dollars, and you leave your car here for as long as you need."

"Do they think you might not return alive?"

"Most amusing. The plane leaves in fifty minutes. The lady said we could have the last two seats. But there isn't anyone else here."

We pulled our bags out of the car, hunched ourselves against the weather, and dashed into the terminal.

"I hope the plane's flying in these conditions," I said. "Maybe the other passengers think they'll cancel it? How many seats does it have?"

"Nine."

"Nine?"

"Ten, if you include the pilot."

"Pilot? One pilot?"

"Yep. How many do you want?" asked Fiona.

"Um, the tiniest commercial plane we've flown in had seventeen seats and two pilots."

"This one's going to be the same, only smaller."

"What happens if the pilot has a heart attack during the flight?"

"The most experienced passenger takes the wheel, or we crash."

I paused and tapped my finger on my mouth.

I still hadn't told Fiona about my cow-bothering, thirty-minute flying lesson.

Am I the most experienced passenger? Will I have to be the backup pilot?

I hoped the actual pilot turned out to be suitably young and fit.

We checked in our backpack and tent and walked through to the gate.

Fiona read the guidebook. Other travellers arrived and occupied seats.

Fiona rotated her wrist and glanced at her watch.

"We're supposed to take off in ten minutes."

"Perhaps it's too windy to fly?" I said.

The guidebook's pages ruffled, as the glass doors leading to the tarmac opened, and a young man entered, wearing a brown sheepskin flying jacket. I imagined him to have arrived from the set of *Those Magnificent Men in Their Flying Machines*. He pushed his glasses onto his head and surveyed the waiting passengers.

"Good morning, everyone," he said. "Welcome to your flight to Stewart Island. I'm Robin, your pilot across the Foveaux Strait today."

This was a novel experience. I'd never heard a pilot introduce himself in the terminal.

I assessed his fitness, to ensure he was unlikely to require the most experienced passenger's help during the flight. The fact he wore shorts in this weather contributed to him meeting my approval.

"Bit of a blowy one today," he said, "but nothing we haven't experienced before. Please make your way out to the runway and enter the plane via the rear door."

Fiona held on to me. We splashed through puddles and followed Robin to a white aeroplane with two silver propellers. Red, cursive writing on its side advertised the Invercargill—Stewart Island Connection. Two doors folded back along its body, one in front of the wings for the pilot, and one near the tail for the passengers.

I reckoned this might be the only plane the airline possessed.

I ducked my head to enter, squeezed along the aisle to a seat at the front, and twisted around to smile at Fiona. Other passengers took their seats, and Robin slammed the door.

He sat directly in front of me behind the yoke, turned, and addressed us.

"Lifejacket's under your seat. Everybody buckled in? Let's go."

We had just received the safety demonstration.

Robin donned a headset.

I heard the drone of turning propellers.

Raindrops ran up Robin's windscreen.

I could see his lips move, as he spoke through his mouthpiece.

The plane moved down the runway, semi-circled, and stopped.

Robin's windscreen wipers flapped, but they couldn't keep up with the downpour.

The propeller noise increased.

I gripped the seat arms and tensed all my muscles.

I can't believe he's taking off in this weather.

The push against my rear informed me our speed had increased, and I leant back while we left the ground.

My internal organs rearranged themselves, as the plane dropped and rose again.

The engine noise amplified, the plane bounced, and it lurched to the left, then the right. Robin tapped his fingers on the yoke.

I recapped my flying lesson with Doug, and observed Robin carefully, in case I had to take over.

The plane plummeted, and my stomach rose to the roof. The seatbelt pulled on my lap. I searched for a sick bag.

I hope Fiona's okay, but if I turn around to check on her, I'll throw up.

I glimpsed land. It disappeared and materialised again, as the plane roller-coastered.

With a bang, we hit the runway and taxied to a stop. I wanted to reach over and shake Robin's hand.

He opened the passenger door, and I panted short, shallow breaths of fresh air.

Fiona stepped out and held her stomach. She puffed her cheeks, and her face shone whiter than a Rumbelows' appliance showroom.

"Your transport to town," said Robin. He pointed with his arm at a minibus with a luggage trailer behind it.

I watched the driver pull baggage from the plane and drop it into the trailer.

I didn't want to climb into any more moving vehicles, so I waited in the fresh air.

The sun came out.

"Yaay," said Fiona, "it's going to be a nice day."

We removed our hoods and allowed the rays to warm our heads.

The bus driver indicated we should board. As we took our seats, rain pelted on the windows.

"Far out," said Fiona. "Rain, sun, rain, all within five minutes."

≈≈≈

The owner of Stewart Island Backpackers pegged out laundry on a rotary clothesline. She used four pegs for each item, regardless of whether she hung up a double sheet or a handkerchief.

"Hello," I said, "do you have anywhere we could pitch our tent?"

She smiled, with two clothes pegs clenched between her teeth.

"Goog horr-hing."

Shaggy blonde hair blew around her ruddy red face.

She removed the pegs.

"Sorry. I meant, good morning." She laughed. "I'm Raylene; this is our camping area." She pointed at a patch of grass which overlooked a bay. "How long did you want to stay?"

"One night, please. We're here for a quick visit."

"No problem. It's five dollars for both of you. Pitch your tent under the tall hedge; it'll shelter you from the wind."

A sudden lash of rain pelted exposed skin. We swivelled and turned our backs to it. Raylene abandoned her laundry and ran into a nearby glasshouse. Fiona and I followed.

We observed the scene from the open door.

Grey clouds covered the wind-whipped whitecaps. Fishing boats danced at anchor, as if they were marionettes operated by a celestial hand. Raylene's clothesline spun as fast as the Tasmanian Devil cartoon.

Helplessly, we watched the washing basket skate along the path, pirouette gracefully, upend itself, and vomit pillowcases over the lawn.

The sun came out.

"Damn," said Raylene, "I'll have to wash those again."

She strode out of the greenhouse and gathered her linen.

"Weather's changeable here, isn't it?" I said.

"That's Stewart Island," said Raylene. "If you don't enjoy the climate, wait five minutes."

"Let's erect the tent before it rains again," said Fiona.

We yanked it out of its packet, and I banged in pegs with a stone. Fiona inserted the poles into the tubes that formed the roof. She laid out spongy roll mats and sleeping bags.

"I'm pegging out extra guy ropes again," I shouted as the gusts increased.

Fiona popped her head out.

"What an amazing view. I think I'll sleep with the tent door open tonight."

I finished nailing the tent to Stewart Island and turned around.

The puppeteer had completed the performance, and the small craft bobbed gently on the dark blue water. Green bushes framed the view, and single-storey, white houses peeped through the trees surrounding the bay.

Fiona lay on her front in the tent with the guidebook opened in front of her.

"What's this place called?" I asked.

"The settlement's named Halfmoon Bay," she said. "It's the only town on the island."

"I love the way New Zealanders call any group of houses a town. In England we'd call this a village."

Raindrops spat on my head, and I jumped inside the tent with her. We lay together, and watched the boats perform their highland jig. I could see Raylene's clothesline rotate like a playground roundabout, the white sheets tangling in its lines. The tent sides flapped gently.

"This is cosy," said Fiona.

"I wonder if her washing ever dries."

"It must do, or she wouldn't hang it out. It won't take long in this breeze."

"What's next?"

"Let's grab some lunch," said Fiona, "and go for a walk along the beaches. I saw a poster advertising a tour to view wild kiwis, but its 230 dollars each. We can't afford that. Plus, I think it only runs in the summer."

"I must see a kiwi while we're here. We could create our own tour to find them. We'll search in the bushes on our walk."

"They're nocturnal," said Fiona. "They hide in burrows during the day."

"Let's have a look for burrows, then. And when we find one, we'll mark the spot, and return at night to see the kiwi come out."

Fiona rolled her eyes.

"Okay. Whatever keeps you happy."

Pleasant sunshine warmed the grass. Fiona stuffed the guidebook in her jacket pocket, and I zipped up the tent. The pillowcases fluttered on the line. Fiona took my hand, and we strolled along the road to town.

≈≈≈

"Why not," said Fiona. She studied a menu Blu-tacked in a shop window.

"Why not what?"

"Why not. It's the name of the café. But its closed. And there isn't a food menu, only drinks. It says you have to bring your own food."

I laughed. "I've heard of bringing your own wine to a restaurant, but bringing your own food?"

We bought provisions at a mini-market. As the weather remained stable for five minutes, we sat on a bench and ate them.

Fiona bit a chunk from a Granny Smith and read the guidebook.

"This is interesting," she said. "Stewart Island has just four kilometres of road."

"It'd hardly be worth having a car."

"Most of the vehicles here look pretty elderly."

"You can't just pop down the local Ford dealer and buy a new one, can you?" I said. "I don't know how you transport a car to the island."

"Shall we walk? The rain's holding off."

We ambled along a country lane straight out of a *Famous Five* novel. A light breeze rustled the trees, and blackberry bushes covered the verges. Fiona picked and ate some berries. Her fingers turned purple. She popped one between my lips.

"These are amazing," I said. "So sweet and tasty."

"They're a noxious weed," said Fiona. "They're not native to New Zealand."

She handed me another palmful of noxious weeds, and I stuffed them in my mouth.

A man with a long, grey beard stood next to a light blue Landrover, with its bonnet open.

"Good morning," I said.

He nodded, turned away, and leant into the engine.

If we were in a *Famous Five* novel, here was the suspicious smuggler.

"He didn't seem friendly, did he?" I said to Fiona when we were out of earshot.

"The locals are wary of outsiders, remember."

We ducked down a track, through trees, and strolled hand-in-hand beside transparent sea, the solitary occupants of a wide crescent-moon of white sand.

A wooden handrail bracketed the path's route over a bluff. Stone steps led into bush, and we arrived on the other side at a small bay with an unnerving signpost.

"Dead Man Beach," read Fiona.

"Take my photo," I said, and I splayed on my back next to the sign.

Fiona giggled and snapped me.

"Simon, you're nuts," she said. "It's a horrible name for a beautiful, wild stretch of sand."

We stood and watched white-capped waves march across the horizon beyond moored fishing boats.

"Wait here, I'm going to search for kiwi burrows."

I dived into the bushes behind the beach. Fiona placed her hands on her hips and waited for me.

Rough shrubbery obstructed my efforts, so I pushed it aside, crouched down, and investigated indentations in the ground.

I lay on my stomach, peered into a narrow hole, and moved aside to allow sunlight to shine in.

A short distance down a passage, four eyes peeked back at me.

25. JUST ONE CORNETTO

I looked up and stared in again.

Two small, fluffy birds wedged together at the rear of the hollow, like identical cuddly toys on a shelf at Hamley's.

I stood, and beckoned Fiona with my entire arm. "I've found some. Two kiwis."

"You're joking. Let me see."

"Here. In this hole. Lie on the ground and look towards the back."

Fiona pushed a bush aside, lay on the dune and peered down the hole.

"Did you see them?" I asked. "Pass me the camera, quick."

Fiona knelt and smiled. "Simon, those aren't kiwis."

"They're not?"

"Nope. Those birds are penguins."

"Penguins?" I said. "Are you sure?"

I poked my nose in the burrow again.

"I'm sure," she said. "Those are baby Little Blue penguins, waiting in their homes for their parents to return with fish."

The Little Blue babies blinked at me.

"Here's another burrow," said Fiona. "And another."

I stood up and looked around. Penguin holes covered the dune, concealed by low bushes.

I lay down again and switched on the camera.

"You can't photograph them," said Fiona. "Remember what the Oamaru ranger told us, not to stick cameras into penguin burrows."

"We'd better check the rest of the holes, to make sure none of them contain kiwis."

Fiona took my hand. "I'm sure they won't. We should return to town; we don't want to be lost in the bush after dark."

I replaced the Olympus in my pack, and we retraced our steps to the beach.

≈≈≈

"I'm hungry after that walk," said Fiona. "And cold."

"Let's go to the pub. It's the only place here which provides evening meals."

The South Sea Hotel advertised itself as The Most Southerly Pub in the World. We walked up to the doors of the double-fronted, white, wooden building, which overlooked the water. I wondered how many customers ever benefited from the beer garden in the changeable weather.

Three weather-beaten men perched on stools at one end of the bar. They all wore black-and-red, checked, flannelette shirts and black beanie hats, as if they'd agreed on a uniform.

They discussed fish, or the lack of them.

A barman entered from a rear room.

"Are you serving food tonight?" I asked.

"Yep," he said. "The kitchen's just opened."

He pulled out a dog-eared piece of card and laid it in front of me.

"D'you fancy fish and chips?" I asked Fiona. "That's what I'm having."

"Good idea," she said. "The salt air makes you hungry for fish."

"Two fish and chips, please," I said. "Is it local?"

"Course it's local." One of the men at the end of the bar addressed me. "Probably caught by one of these two buggers."

He raised his glass to his companions, who laughed and clinked their drinks against it.

"Where are you from?" asked the man who'd spoken. "You've got a funny accent."

His brown moustache sat between red cheeks with broken veins.

"I'm from England," I said.

He tipped back the end of a glass of beer and thumped it on the counter. The barman refilled it.

"Shit," he said. "You're a long way from home. I didn't think you poms went further than Spain."

"I'm a local," said Fiona. "I'm from New Zealand."

"New Zealand?" said another of the men. "I haven't been there in twenty years."

They all laughed at this remark. I joined in, though I didn't understand the joke.

The barman wrote our order on a pad and handed it to another member of staff. "Down here on Stewart Island," he said, "we think of ourselves as separate from New Zealand. There's even a campaign for independence."

He lowered his voice. "I think it's a bit tongue in cheek. But I'm not a local; I'm not from here originally."

"How long have you lived in Halfmoon Bay?" I asked.

"Thirty years. I met a Stewart Island lady while I studied at college in Christchurch, and she dragged me back."

"I reckon after thirty years you could consider yourself a local," I said.

"Nope," said the barman. "They still call me Tom the mainlander."

"Would you like a drink?" I asked Fiona.

"Could I have a hot chocolate? I need to warm up on the inside."

"One hot chocolate, please. And I'll have a twelve of Speights."

Tom the mainlander poured my beer. We selected a table, and he brought Fiona's hot chocolate.

She sipped it.

"Wow, Simon. This is yummy."

She sipped again.

"I can't believe, in this remote corner of the world, I've found the best hot chocolate I've ever drunk."

She took another sip and picked up a marshmallow placed in the saucer.

"Skrark?" inquired something behind her.

A large, white cockatoo climbed the outside of a cage. It tugged at the bars and used its beak to pull itself up.

It turned its head upside down and inspected us.

"Hello," said Fiona. "You're a long way from Australia."

Tom brought our meals on oval plates. They were too small for the battered fish, which stuck off the ends. A small salad squeezed on the side. Some of it fell on the table.

"He'll sit on your arm if you offer it," he said.

I realized he meant the cockatoo.

Fiona stood up and picked some sunflower seeds out of the cockatoo's bowl. She placed them in her flat hand and held her arm out straight. An itch behind his right ear briefly distracted the bird.

He turned his head to one side.

He turned it back again and stepped onto Fiona's elbow.

She dropped her arm before raising it again. The cockatoo flapped his wings and successfully remained attached.

"Woah," said Fiona. "I wasn't ready for him to be so heavy."

The bird walked along Fiona's arm towards her hand. He bent his head to her palm, collected some seeds in his beak, balanced on one claw, and used the other to stuff them in his mouth.

The seed pods dropped over the floor where they joined the previous day's collection.

Fiona scratched his head.

The sound of crunching continued.

He examined Fiona's hand, to see if it contained any more seeds. Finding it didn't, he used his beak like an ice-pick to mountaineer up her sleeve.

"I'll put you back on your cage," said Fiona. "My arm's tired."

Fiona attached the cockatoo to the cage as if she were hanging up a coat. He grasped the bars in his claws, turned his head around, and scrutinized her, before commencing a gymnastic display for our benefit.

"Come and eat your fish," I said. "It'll get cold."

≈≈≈

"We should've brought a torch. I can't see my hand in front of my face. How are we going to find the tent?"

"Shut your eyes for a bit," I said. "Let them adjust to the dark."

We closed our eyes and re-opened them. I saw shadowy outlines.

We felt our way to the tent. A gentle breeze flapped the fly sheet.

"This is cosy, with the wind," said Fiona, as we lay in our sleeping bags.

"So long as it's nothing like Mount Cook."

"I've enjoyed Stewart Island," said Fiona, "but I'm glad we're leaving in the morning. It's too isolated for me."

"I'm so disappointed we didn't see a kiwi. Now where am I going to find one?"

A brief shower spattered.

It stopped, and the wind stilled.

I heard an unfamiliar bird call.

"Peeooo, peeooo, peeooo."

I turned my ear and listened.

"Peeooo, peeooo, peeooo."

"Is that a kiwi?" I asked.

Fiona snuggled against me.

The minibus windscreen wipers flapped at full speed. I'd no idea how the driver discerned where the road ran, but as we hadn't seen any other traffic this didn't seem to matter.

"I hope the plane can land in this weather," said Fiona.

Rain eased to drizzle, and a disc of sun blurred through the clouds.

The little plane landed and circled on the tarmac. We exchanged places with the incoming passengers.

I recognized the pilot and said, "Hello, Robin." He had headphones on while he scribbled notes on a clipboard, and he didn't hear me.

Robin taxied the plane to the end of the runway and turned around.

The rain drummed on his windscreen.

He sped up, and we took off.

I gazed out of the window and couldn't tell where the grey sky ended, and the savage sea began.

"Queenstown," said Fiona, "is somewhere I haven't visited since I was about ten years old."

Hordes of tourists in tents, caravans, and campervans milled around the campsite. The manager directed us to an empty patch of grass, and I shook out the tent, spread it in a square shape, and stuck pegs in the ground. Fiona climbed in and smoothed out our sleeping bags. I gazed past rows of pine trees, to a backdrop of a deep, navy-blue lake pierced by sheer mountains.

"Why is it called Queenstown?" I asked.

"Early settlers reckoned this spot was so beautiful, it could only be fit for a Queen."

"The guidebook mentioned it's the adventure sports capital of New Zealand."

Fiona poked her head out and stood up.

"We've the rest of the day here. Although I'm not sure we'll have enough time to do the jet boating or white-water rafting."

"Or the money."

"Let's walk into town and find something we can afford. It's crazy, isn't it? I start work on Monday, and we'll have money, but we'll have no time to do anything. Now we've the time, but we've no money."

Queenstown's main street consisted entirely of opportunities to deplete a wallet of its contents. Shops advertised bungy jumping, rafting, and jet boat riding. In recognition of a dusting of snow on the mountains, staff in a ski shop arranged puffy clothing and boots, and a sign advertised an Autumn sale.

We stopped and investigated the window of The Lakefront Activity Centre.

A young lady in a red polo shirt strode out of the shop and joined us on the pavement. She grasped a wodge of leaflets and shoved one at me.

"Would you like to do the white-water rafting?" she said, in an Irish accent. "We're offering ten percent discount today."

She tossed her long, black hair over her shoulders.

I folded my arms.

"How much is it?"

"Usually 200 dollars," she said. "But I can offer you 180 dollars, if you book right now."

I contemplated the leaflet. A bright-yellow raft tumbled down rapids, with six young, open-mouthed people in it, wearing black helmets.

I turned to Fiona. "D'you think we could afford that?"

"Is it 180 dollars for both of us?" she asked.

"That's the price each," said the saleswoman. "So, 360 dollars in total."

"Sorry, Simon," said Fiona. "We can't."

"Do you sell other tours?" I asked.

"Bungy jumping?" The Irish lady selected another leaflet and held it out. "You'll ride by minibus up the Shotover River, you'll jump from a high bridge, touch the water, and bungy up again. It's amazing. I've done it so many times."

"How much does the bungy jumping cost?"

"It's 225 dollars normally. I can offer it to you for 200 dollars, but you have to book right now."

"Each?"

"Each."

"Um, anything else?"

"There's the jet boat along the river. That's a thrilling experience."

A third leaflet joined my collection, with a photograph of a bright red speedboat containing a group of screaming passengers.

"How much is the jet boating?"

"It's 250 dollars, but if you book right now, I can offer it to you for 225 dollars."

"Each?"

"Each."

"Thanks, we can't afford any of these."

We strolled further along the pavement.

A second shop window offered a similar display.

With similar leaflets.

With similar prices.

"Queenstown's ridiculously expensive," I said. "How does anyone enjoy anything here?"

"I can see the Tourist Information Centre ahead," said Fiona. "Let's investigate what they suggest."

We stepped up into a single-storey modern building, and I approached the middle-aged lady behind the desk. Her badge identified her as Elizabeth Jackson.

"Are there any tours here which don't cost hundreds of dollars?" I asked her. "Everything seems designed for millionaires."

Elizabeth laughed, picked up grey, plastic spectacles, and pushed them on her nose.

"I'm sure we can find something. Come with me."

She led us to a rack of leaflets which included the same ones as the Irish girl had offered us.

"How about a trip on a paddle steamer?"

She pulled out a single page pamphlet, with a photo of an old-fashioned boat on the front. The picture displayed smiling passengers in 1960s clothing, enjoying the sun on its upper deck.

"How much money is the paddle steamer?" I asked.

"It's 36 dollars each, including tea or coffee and a cake."

"We can afford that," said Fiona. "We can eat the cake for lunch."

"Thanks, Elizabeth. That's much more in our budget. Anything else?"

She laughed at my use of her name badge. "Call me Liz."

She showed me another leaflet.

"There's the gondola," she said.

"Gondola?"

I had a vision of an Italian man, with a waxed black moustache, stripy shirt, and straw hat, poling us across the lake, singing 'Just One Cornetto'.

"It's a cable car ride up the mountain," said Liz. "At the top there's the Skyline Restaurant, which has views over the lake. You could watch the sunset over a romantic dinner."

I imagined sitting opposite my gorgeous Fiona, at a white linen setting, a single rose in a vase between us, holding hands across the table, while the orange glow of the sunset reflected in the lake and lit up the mountains.

"How much does the gondola cost?" I asked Liz.

"It's 150 dollars each, including the meal."

The image of the silver-served romantic dinner evaporated.

Liz noticed my disappointment.

"For 35 dollars, you can ride up, admire the view, and come straight down again."

"I think we'll just ride the gondola," I said to Fiona. "We could buy a take-away and eat it by the lake."

"Oh," said Liz. "And next to the gondola is the Kiwi Park."

My eyes opened wide.

"Kiwi Park? Are you serious? D'you mean a park with real live kiwis?"

26. TURKEY BASTER

My mouth hung open. I turned to Fiona and back to Liz.

"This Kiwi Park," I said. "Will there be kiwi birds strolling around on the grass?"

Liz laughed. "It's called the Kiwi Park, and they've got kiwis, but it's not what you're thinking. Kiwis are nocturnal."

"Oh yes, of course they are," I said. "So the park's open at night?"

"No, no, it's open during the daytime," said Liz. "The Park has a dark enclosure, which fools the kiwis into believing it's night-time. You'll understand when you see it. You could go there after the paddle steamer."

I bounced from my left foot to my right.

"We're going to see kiwis, Fiona. Actual, real, live kiwis. I'll be able to keep my promise to Dad."

"All right, Simon, calm down," said Fiona. "I'm happy for you."

She turned to Liz. "Where does the paddle steamer depart from?"

"The wharf at the end of the street." She glanced at a clock. "You'd better go. It leaves in twenty minutes."

≈≈≈

Fiona jumped as a loud whistle announced the TSS Earnslaw's imminent departure, and a lazy plume of smoke issued from its funnel. We paid our fares at a kiosk and stepped on board. Middle-aged and elderly people milled around the decks. We were the youngest passengers by about forty years.

I watched a crew member cast off a rope. The pleasant rhythmic puff-puff-puff of the engine increased as the paddle wheels rotated.

"Good morning, ladies and gentlemen," announced a loudspeaker. "Welcome to the TSS Earnslaw, the last remaining passenger-carrying, coal-fired steamship in the southern hemisphere. In the unlikely event of an emergency, there are two exits, one directly over the left side, and one directly over the right."

The pensioners laughed at the captain's well-rehearsed speech.

"Life jackets are contained at various points on the deck, and in the cabin, marked with the words 'life jackets'."

More polite laughter.

"I'll be pointing out some sights as we cruise. For now, please enjoy the refreshments served in the main cabin."

The puff-puff-puff continued, as the pensioners queued for tea and cakes.

We hung over the rail and gazed into the lake. A fjord-like setting of mountains soared above us on both sides.

"I think," I said, "New Zealand's the most beautiful country I've seen in the world."

Fiona took my hand. "I'm so glad you like it here. I hope it all works out for us."

Her lips pressed together.

"I do miss England," she said. "The castles, and the historic homes. And the shopping. It sounds crazy, but I'm even longing for the choice of groceries at Sainsbury's."

"You and your shopping. We need to earn more money before we can buy anything."

Another loud hoot for the benefit of the hard-of-hearing, followed by the captain's voice.

"We'll be heading up Lake Wakatipu towards Walter Peak. The mountain range you can see on your left is called The Remarkables."

Small patches of snow lay in gullies. Rugged peaks topped pine-forested slopes that plunged into the lake and were devoid of any sign of human habitation. I watched small, low clouds float below the mountain tops.

The captain's voice echoed again.

"Lake Wakatipu is New Zealand's longest lake, and its third largest. It reaches 380 metres deep, and its bottom is well below sea level."

The steamer puffed, hooted, and turned 180 degrees.

An older couple approached and leant on the rail beside us. The man wore a red and white scarf decorated with an English flag. He wiped crumbs from his hands with a napkin.

"It's a bit like Scotland, isn't it, Geoffrey?" said the lady.

"Nope," said Geoffrey. He adjusted his flat cap and chewed an unlit pipe.

"Reminds me of Loch Ness," said his wife.

"Nothing like it," said Geoffrey.

"Yes, it is. The high mountains, the deep water. You could imagine a monster living in this lake, too."

"Can't compare them," said Geoffrey.

"Go on, what's different?"

"I'll tell you what's different, Margaret. No bloody Scotsmen here, with their stupid outfits and their sodding bagpipes, sounding like a sack full of strangled parrots."

"What d'you have against Scotsmen?"

"Nothing, Margaret. Nothing a good game of football won't cure. We're playing them in a couple of months in the European Championships. Haven't been drawn against them for seven years. We beat them last time, and we're going to beat the haggis-eating caber-tossers again."

"Geoffrey, can't you enjoy our holiday and stop going on about football?"

"Seven years, Margaret. Seven years."

Fiona pulled me away. "I'm hungry," she said. "Let's fetch our cup of tea and cake."

≈≈≈

The young lady at the Kiwi Park smiled at us. She wore a buff green shirt displaying the park's logo, and her brown hair was tied back in a ponytail.

She tore two tickets from a pad. "Seven dollars each, please."

I hesitated.

"I want to confirm. You do have real, live kiwi birds?"

She pushed her glasses onto her head.

"Of course we do. There are five here at the moment."

"And we're definitely going to see them today?"

"Yes, in our nocturnal kiwi house. We keep it dark during daytime, so the kiwis think it's night."

"Can we photograph them?"

"Um, you can't use flash, obviously. So your photos might not turn out. You could buy a postcard of a kiwi from our shop?"

"Stop asking stupid questions and pay the entrance fee," said Fiona. "This is your best chance of seeing a kiwi, so let's get on with it."

"All right, all right. I'm just making sure."

The lady took my money and handed me a leaflet.

"Follow the signs to the nocturnal house. And have a look at our other exhibits, the keas, kererus and wekas. Oh, and the park closes in one hour, at 4:30."

"Thanks," I said. I pulled Fiona outside through a rear exterior door. She stopped at a notice board, which depicted brown outline illustrations of various birds dotted around a map of the site. I waved the back of my hand at it twice.

"I've seen all of those other birds in the wild," I said. "I just want to see the kiwis. Here we are, the nocturnal house." I read a sign. "Hold the handrail and let your eyes adjust to the light. No torches or flash photography. Close the door behind you."

Fiona pushed the swing door, and we entered darkness.

"Simon, I can't see anything at all," said Fiona.

"Why are you whispering?"

"I don't know. So's not to scare the kiwis, I suppose."

"Close your eyes tight," I said, "count to twenty, then open them."

I felt along the wall for the handrail and guided Fiona into the viewing area.

"I can see something," I said.

"Me too. Plants."

We peered through a glass wall, into a display of tree ferns and low shrubs. The darkness coloured them various shades of grey, as if we were in the night scene of a dramatic 1950s murder mystery film.

"Can you see any kiwis?" asked Fiona.

"Nope. Let's allow our eyes to adjust more."

We stood and stared at the grey.

"Is something moving near the back?" I asked.

"Where?"

"There, under that fern."

"I can't see where you're pointing."

We waited. If the kiwis were present, they were aiming for first prize at hide-and-seek.

"This is a rip-off," I said. "We've been in here fifteen minutes and haven't seen any kiwis. I don't think there are any here. It's all a big con."

"Calm down," said Fiona. "I'll ask the reception lady what we're supposed to do."

"Okay, I'll wait here, in case they break cover while you're away."

Fiona felt her way out of the door.

She returned a minute later and ran her hands over my front.

"Erm, I don't think we should get frisky in here."

"I'm not getting frisky. I can't see where you are. My eyes need to adjust again. Have you spotted any kiwis yet?"

"No. What did the lady say?"

"She's coming in a minute."

We watched the grey trees. There was a marked lack of kiwis.

Fiona grabbed my hand. "Something's moving. At the back. Oh, it's the lady."

We noticed the outline of the receptionist enter through a door at the rear. She walked towards us, reached under a bush, and grabbed a round, fluffy ball.

She placed it in front of us.

I crouched in the twilight and watched, entranced.

The kiwi stood on two stumpy feet and prodded the ground in front of it with its long, turkey-baster beak.

It walked with jerky motions, tap-tap-tapping, as if it were a blind man walking with a cane.

I put my head on one side and furrowed my brow.

This bird lacked something fundamental.

Wings.

I'd never seen a bird without wings.

It looked like it should have a pair, but they weren't present.

The kiwi drilled its beak into the ground from side to side, pulled it out, and extracted a worm. It wiggled its head briskly and drew the worm into its mouth.

It stalked off towards the rear of the glass cage and evaporated into the undergrowth.

We waited, but it didn't reappear.

"Let's go," whispered Fiona. "The park'll be closing, and you want to buy a kiwi postcard for your dad."

≈≈≈

We blinked in the afternoon sunlight and entered the gift shop.

"Such a special experience," I said. I selected a postcard and turned it over and back again. "That's one of my life goals ticked off. It's a shame I couldn't take a photo."

"Instead of going directly to the gondola," said Fiona, "shall we walk around the lake for a couple of hours? It'd be best to be at the top of the mountain for sunset. We don't want to get there too soon."

"Let's buy dinner, sit by the lake, and eat it."

We found a pizza shop, ordered a Hawaiian to share, and carried it down to the water.

I ripped the lid off the box and used it as my plate.

"It's soggy," said Fiona.

"I agree. Not as good as the food on Stewart Island."

"Cooked from frozen. Typical tourist-location fare."

The sun descended towards the mountain tops, and Fiona shivered.

I put my arm around her. "Come on," I said, "let's ride this gondola."

≈≈≈

The cable car ticket man raised his eyebrows.

"You just want to ride up and down again?"

"Err, yes. Is that okay?"

"You don't want dinner?"

"Thanks, we already ate."

The little, four-person cable cars reminded me of French ski-lifts. We stepped through the double doors, and they slid closed behind us. The gondola lurched away from the platform and ascended through a long clearing in the trees running up the side of the mountain. Fiona pointed over my shoulder. I swivelled my head.

"Gosh," she said. "The boats on the lake look so small already. You can see the paddle steamer against the wharf. It's like a child's bath toy."

"And the lake and mountains," I said. "This must be one of most romantic views in the world."

We reached the top, stepped out of the gondola, and entered the Skyline Restaurant.

I opened my eyes wide and gasped.

The dining experience laid out before us wasn't quite what I'd envisaged.

27. EMERGENCY EXIT

My first impression of the dining room at the gondola's summit was a flashback to the feeding trough of my school dining hall.

Hundreds of tourists milled around a long buffet table. They fought for space and lunged over each other to plunder the best goodies.

I observed one man waltzing between the tables, trying to find somewhere to sit. Food pyramided his plate, as if there was about to be a natural disaster and this was the last meal he'd ever eat. Some chips dropped off as he passed, and the diner behind him squished them underfoot.

This wasn't the romantic candlelit dinner I'd imagined. It reminded me of Watford Gap motorway services, on a sunny August Bank Holiday Monday.

"I'm glad we didn't spend a hundred dollars on this experience," said Fiona. "I would have felt ripped off.

"I always say that places with a magnificent view don't have to try too hard with the food."

We stepped outside onto a small balcony area and escaped the Roman orgy.

I snuggled up to Fiona, as the sunset reflected on The Remarkable Mountains. The edge of the lake darkened, and pinpricks of light illuminated where tiny settlements bordered the water.

I pointed. "Look at the reflection of Queenstown's lights."

"It's so pretty," said Fiona. She nuzzled against me.

One by one, stars twinkled above the mountains, and Fiona showed me how to find the Southern Cross, a constellation unfamiliar to northern hemisphere astronomers. I identified the astral hunter, Orion. He was performing a headstand, a gymnastics position I hadn't realised was within his capabilities.

Fiona held me tight. "I'm getting cold," she said.

We entered the cable car and rocked gently down the mountain.

≈≈≈

I awoke to the weird sensation after a chilly night camping, where your body is toasty warm, but your face feels as if you've stuffed it in a freezer.

Frost decorated long strands of grass which the campsite mower had missed.

We huffed thick breath clouds. Neighbouring campers prepared breakfast wearing woolly hats and gloves.

Fiona rubbed her hands on her upper arms. "Far out," she said. "That must have been the coldest camping I've ever experienced."

I bent over and gathered tent pegs. Condensation on their metal moistened my hands. I stood straight and gazed at the lake.

"Look at the mist over the water," I said. "It's like a scene from King Arthur."

"Very nice," said Fiona. "Hurry with the tent; I need to turn the car heater on."

She sat in the driver's seat, shut the car door, and turned the key.

Fiona accelerated through remote farming country, where autumn trees lined the route in russet tinctures. Roadside fruit stalls heralded a settlement named Cromwell, which overlooked an attractive, long, thin lake. Fiona slowed, as we passed the speed limit sign.

"Everything's so modern in this town," I said. "Is it new?"

"Yep. The old Cromwell's under the lake."

"Under the lake? What happened?"

I had a vision of a biblical disaster, with a Moses-like prophet holding out a wooden staff, commanding the waters to retreat.

"The farmers needed a new irrigation reservoir for this area, as they grow a lot of fruit. A few years ago, they dammed the Clutha River to form Lake Dunstan, and flooded the valley, the town, the houses, everything. I understand if the water level's low, you can hear the old church bell ringing."

I leant back and frowned.

"That's so sad," I said. "What about all the people who lost their homes and their memories?"

"It was a significant event in the news. I remember Dad's vocal opposition."

Aqua blue water sparkled in the morning sun. I stared at the opaque reservoir and tried to imagine a drowned chapel, the bell swinging to welcome parishioners who would never arrive.

Thirty minutes later, we entered another lakeside settlement backed by rugged, low hills.

"This town's called Wanaka," said Fiona. "It used to be a sleepy farming service centre, but it's becoming a second Queenstown."

Construction workers unpacked tools from trucks, in a new lakeside subdivision. Diggers and concrete mixers insulted the scenery with their industrial din.

We passed a collection of brightly-painted buildings, leaning at drunken angles.

"What's that?" I asked. "If those are new houses, the builders were on drugs."

"Wanaka's Puzzling World," said Fiona. "I haven't been there since I was a kid. Shall we have a look?"

We entered a car park and stopped between a campervan and a tour bus.

Another camper pulled off the road behind us and parked alongside.

Car doors slammed, and children shouted.

"What's the attraction of Puzzling World?" I asked. "It seems popular."

"Wait and see."

The ticket lady greeted us.

"Good morning. Where are you two from?"

"Hokitika," I said.

"Oh, you're locals," said the lady.

Yes! I'm not a loopy.

"My cousin lives in Hokitika," she said. "Jean Finnegan. Do you know her?"

"Yep," said Fiona. "She's one of our neighbours in the valley."

"Small world," said the lady.

She pointed to a door behind her.

"Start your tour here and follow the signs."

Fiona held the door for me. I entered and placed my palms flat on the wall.

"I feel dizzy," I said. "The room's not square."

"It's an illusion; that's the point."

I struggled to keep my balance and embraced a pillar, as if I were a passenger on the Dover to Calais ferry during a particularly rough crossing.

A pool table stood in the centre of the floor. Fiona struck the white ball with a cue. It rolled away and back towards her.

"I feel sick," I said. "This isn't right; the table looks flat."

"Let's go into the next room."

A ladder slanted against one wall. Fiona stood on the bottom rung and leant out at an impossible angle.

"I'm not sure I can cope with this," I said. "I need to hold on to something."

I sat in a chair mounted on rails against the wall. It slid upwards, defying gravity.

"I have to leave, before I throw up," I said.

I wobbled to a door marked Exit, pushed it, put my hands on my knees, bent over, and inhaled deep breaths of beautiful, fresh, horizontal air.

"I don't want to go in there again," I said. "What else can we do here? What's this castle?"

"It's a maze," said Fiona.

"I think my tummy can cope with a maze."

Fiona read the instructions. "We have to reach the four corner turrets in any order and find the central courtyard. From there we can exit via the gift shop. If we're stuck there are emergency exits."

I gazed at the wooden towers.

"I've heard if you keep turning right in a maze, you'll find the way out," I said.

"It's not right, it's left," said Fiona.

She pushed a door marked 'Start', turned left, jogged up a wooden staircase, and entered the green turret.

"See?" said Fiona. "We have to turn left. We'll be in the shop in five minutes."

We turned left several more times and reached the blue corner.

"This maze isn't hard," said Fiona.

The sun reflected from the roof of the yellow tower.

We walked towards it.

We walked away from it.

We doubled back.

We passed it again.

A middle-aged couple waited in a corner. The man frowned and rested one finger flat on his mouth.

The lady clenched her fists. Her mouth was straight and her eyes wide. She glared at her husband.

"We need to find our way out of here, Ron; we'll miss the bloody bus."

Ron scratched his head and stood on tiptoe to see across the maze.

"We should have turned right under the blue tower," he said.

"Oh, for goodness' sake," said the lady. "Let's use the emergency exit."

"I told you, Carol, we're not using the emergency exit."

"That's your problem. You won't admit when you're beaten."

"I'm not beaten." Ron stood on tiptoe again and rubbernecked left and right. "I'm sure it's this way. Follow me."

Ron strode on through the maze. Carol shook her head, threw her hands in the air, and followed him. For all I knew they could have been in there for days.

We turned left again. And again.

"Fiona, the yellow tower's behind us."

"I know. I think we have to walk away from it to reach it."

We climbed a staircase to an elevated platform in the centre of the maze and stared at the whole labyrinth from above.

Fiona leant out and pointed. "The yellow tower's over there."

She traced a line in the air with her finger.

"Let's go down these stairs, under this platform, around those two left corners, and up the steps by the tower."

She set off, and I followed her. Within thirty seconds, we walked up into the yellow tower. We leant out of a hatch and gawked across the maze, back at the platform we'd come from.

"No idea why we thought it'd be hard," said Fiona.

"The secret seems to be; try not to find the towers."

"Just the red one to go," said Fiona, "and we're done."

I stretched out. In the distance, I saw Ron stride around a corner, perform a left wheel, and march back again. Carol followed, gesticulating wildly.

I pointed. "If we retrace our steps back to the elevated platform, we can view the whole maze again, and figure out the route to the last tower."

"All right," said Fiona, "two left turns, along a straight bit, a right, and we're there."

I followed her, and we arrived back at the green tower.

"This is impossible," said Fiona. "I'm going to climb over a bloody fence in a minute."

"You can't cheat," I said. "You'll spoil the fun. I told you, it's turn right, not left. If we keep taking the right-hand turns, we should pass it eventually."

"Gees, Simon. You sound like that Ron bloke."

We turned right several times and came upon the central courtyard. A sign on a door said 'Shop and Exit'. Fiona pushed it.

"We haven't found the red tower," I said.

"I think I've had enough illusions."

The aroma of fried bacon and onions filled our nostrils.

"Are you hungry?" asked Fiona. "We didn't have breakfast."

I studied a handwritten menu on a chalk board.

My eyebrows raised.

"They sell kiwi burgers," I said. "You can't eat kiwi. Aren't they endangered?"

Fiona laughed.

"A kiwi burger doesn't have a kiwi bird in it. It's a normal burger with a few extras."

"Um, okay. I should taste the local delicacies." I approached the serving hatch. "I'll have a kiwi burger please."

This felt like an odd request.

"And some chips."

"I'll have a milkshake, please," said Fiona.

"Aren't you going to have any food?" I asked her.

"The milkshake'll fill me up. I'll have a few of your chips."

I briefly considered asking for two portions. Usually when Fiona asked for a few of my chips, approximately a third remained for my own consumption.

We sat down, and the waitress brought Fiona's milkshake. She returned a few moments later and placed an edible tower on the table. A meat pattie, salad, cheese, a fried egg, pineapple, and beetroot leached over two halves of a seeded bun. A wooden stick impaled the entire meal from top to bottom.

I stared at the burger, with my palms up. It toppled sideways, and I grabbed it. My hand turned yellow, as egg yolk ran down my fingers.

Fiona picked at my chips.

She smiled and nodded. "That's a kiwi burger, Simon."

I squished the burger between my hands. I took a bite, being careful not to perforate the roof of my mouth with the stick.

Meat juice and purple beetroot dripped down my face, as if I were Count Dracula enjoying a midnight snack.

"Careful of your T-shirt," said Fiona. "Shall I fetch you some more napkins?"

"Buth bleese."

I rotated the burger in my hands.

Fiona returned with the napkins.

"Can you feed me a chip?" I asked. "I can't put the burger down. It'll disintegrate."

Fiona picked up a chip and stuffed it in my mouth.

"Goodness knows how this looks to other diners," she said.

I ate around the perimeter, until a stick-speared circle of burger remained.

My fingers stained purple from the beetroot.

Fiona finished my chips. I'd eaten three of them.

The remaining burger fell apart on my plate, and I picked up individual components. I licked my fingers, pushed my plate to one side, and liquidated an entire pack of serviettes.

"Shall I drive?" I asked.

"Don't forget the Haast Pass is ahead."

"Is it as dangerous as Arthur's Pass?" I asked, "with the one-lane sections, the big trucks, and the rocks dropping on the road?"

"Might be."

The deep, blue, desolate waters of Lake Wanaka stretched away towards distant mountains. White snow patches contrasted against the blue sky, reminding me of photographs on laminated placemats.

The lake petered out at two homes and a petrol station, in a dot of a settlement called Makarora.

"We'd better fill up before we cross the Haast Pass," said Fiona. "We should have done it in Wanaka."

"What would happen if the car ran out of fuel on the pass?" I asked.

"We'd be stuck. Someone would give us a ride. It'd be a long day."

I unclipped the Makarora service station's petrol nozzle. A man in a beanie hat and Wellington boots exited the shop.

"I'll do that," he said.

He tucked his checked shirt into his trousers and confiscated the pump handle.

"Erm, thank you. Fill her up, please."

The man stuck the nozzle in the filler hole. He whistled, as the numbers on the petrol pump dial rotated. I returned to the driver's seat.

"This is like England in the 1970s," I said to Fiona. "I can't recall the last time an attendant filled a car for me."

"It's becoming rarer in New Zealand, too."

The man closed the filler cap.

"Twenty-three dollars please." He studied the car. "You folks local? Doesn't look like a rental."

"We're from Hokitika," said Fiona.

"Hokitika, eh? Do you know Frank Wall?" asked the attendant.

"He's my dad," said Fiona.

"Well, give him my regards," said the man. "Tell him, Vic says hello. He used to give me some good racing tips."

"All right, I will, thanks."

I paid him, and we pulled out. I understood how easy it would be for tourists to exit a remote petrol station on the wrong side of the road.

≈≈≈

Desolate.

Wild.

Wind-blown.

The road passed through open, flat countryside. I changed down a gear, as we began the climb up to the mountain pass. A small, brown car approached. The driver waved, and we returned the greeting.

Left bend.

Right bend.

Left bend.

Tall tree-ferns populated the verges; thick, black stems with lush, monkey-tail fronds at their apex. I glimpsed rushing water in a steep valley to our right.

I swung around a blind corner and stamped on the brake pedal.

"Fiona, what the hell's this man doing standing in the middle of the road?"

28. INTRODUCED PESTS

In the centre of the empty road, a yellow-vested worker leant on a wooden pole, with a circular sign mounted at its top. He slumped, with his eyes closed.

I'd never considered the physical possibility of falling asleep holding a stop sign.

I crawled up to him and started to drive around the sign.

"His sign says 'Stop'," said Fiona, "so you should stop."

I stopped.

The worker continued his slumbers.

I revved the engine.

Fiona wound down the passenger window.

"Excuse me," she shouted.

The man opened his eyes. He gazed around and noticed our car.

He scratched his head, glanced up at the top of his sign, and blinked.

He spoke into a walkie-talkie, waved at us, and spun the sign, which now said 'Go'.

Fiona waved back. We drove on.

"What's he doing, all the way out here by himself?" I asked.

We rounded the next bend.

Two yellow-vested men worked with a large digger. Its arm extended over the valley, and a truck obstructed one side of the road. A triangular, orange sign showed the familiar men-at-work symbol.

The road was missing a semi-circular chunk, as if a kiwi Godzilla had climbed out of the valley and helped itself to a bite of bitumen.

"Landslip," said Fiona.

I braked and inched along the remaining road surface, between the rock-face on our left, and the precipitous drop on our right. I gawked at how little asphalt separated my right tyre from the missing chunk of road.

My clammy hands stuck to the wheel. Orange cones gave the unwarranted impression of safety. The car's right wheel touched one, and it bent. The digger operators hadn't noticed.

I passed the precipice and breathed out. Fiona watched out of the passenger seat, oblivious to how close we'd come to emulating a spectacular scene from a James Bond movie. The part where the music stops, the baddie's car plummets over a cliff, somersaults in silent slow-motion, and explodes spectacularly at the base.

At the next corner, a fourth man waited with another lollipop sign. He waved and spoke into his radio.

I acknowledged his greeting and increased speed.

"Does that happen often?" I asked, "the road slipping away?"

"Sometimes the West Coast Road is closed for days, with towns cut off, until workers clear the debris."

Dense, lush greenery framed the roadway. I expected to see a dinosaur pop its head out from behind one of the giant ferns. We wound along the thin, asphalt ribbon bisecting Jurassic Park. At some point, we re-entered the West Coast, but I couldn't tell which vast, dripping leaf formed the boundary.

A sign indicated a settlement called Haast.

"How far to the glaciers from here?" I asked.

"At least another two hours."

I blinked.

"Two hours? People who live in this Haast place are two hours from Wanaka, and two hours from the glaciers? How many people live at the glaciers?"

"Not many. A hundred?"

"How far is it from the glaciers to Hokitika?"

"Another two hours."

"Haast's two hours from the nearest town in one direction, and four hours in the other? Where do they do their shopping? For instance, if they need a chemist."

"Wanaka, I suppose."

"So, every time you need an aspirin, you have to cross the pass? And if the road's washed away in a landslip, you're stuck."

"Yep. Tough people, us West Coasters."

I paused at the entrance to the longest one-lane bridge I'd seen. No cars approached, so I began the crossing.

A stream rushed along one edge of a wide expanse of gravel riverbed. I glanced left and right as we crossed. I tried to imagine what this must look like, when the river flooded, and covered the gravel from bank to bank.

A truck entered at the other end of the bridge.

The guidebook hadn't provided instructions for this occurrence.

"Now what?" I asked, as the truck grew larger, like a scene from Mad Max.

"It's his right of way," said Fiona.

"How would I know?"

"The sign as we entered the bridge."

"I didn't see a give way sign. I saw two arrows."

"Yep, the red one showed he's allowed to cross first."

"But the truck wasn't on the bridge when we entered."

"I know, but he's bigger than us, so we're not going to argue."

"What do I do, reverse?"

"Nope, pull in here, quick."

She pointed. A small passing space in the middle of the bridge offered an escape. I nipped into it. The truck blasted its horn, and I cringed, as two trailers with the words Trans-West Freighters passed my window.

I gasped at Fiona, and my hands shook on the wheel.

"Anything else to watch out for?"

"Nope. You're good."

The road curved gently, as it followed the sea north, towards the glaciers.

A dead animal lay on the centre white line.

"Was that a cat? Poor puss."

"I didn't see it," said Fiona.

I swerved again. "Another one. What are these dead cats doing here?"

Fiona leant forward and spotted another deceased mammal. "They're not cats; they're possums. They sit on the warm asphalt at night, and they're decapitated by passing cars."

"The possums just want an electric blanket," I said. "Imagine if you sat on a nice, warm bed, and a car chopped your head off."

"They're an introduced pest, remember? Don't feel sorry for them."

"We're just introduced pests ourselves, though, aren't we?"

"I'm not," said Fiona. She grinned. "You might be."

"Hey," I said. "I'm trying to fit in as best I can."

"I know," she said. "Can we stop? I need a pee."

≈≈≈

Two campervans waited for us, as we crossed the one-lane bridge outside Franz Josef Glacier village.

"Black arrow," I said. "Our right of way."

"You're learning," said Fiona.

We entered a driveway and parked next to a sign saying Reception.

I stepped out of the car, breathed in, and felt the cold on the inside of my nostrils. Steam rose from my mouth. I huffed a few times, to see more of it.

"You're lucky," said the campsite manager, as she took our ten-dollar fee. "One pitch left."

We squeezed our tent between several others. I recognized one family from Queenstown.

"D'you want to find some dinner?" I asked Fiona. "This cold air makes me hungry."

We walked a short distance into the town and read a menu outside a hotel.

"This looks good," said Fiona. "Chinese. Yum."

"I wouldn't expect much," I said. "I doubt the chef's from Shanghai."

"Don't be negative. Give it a chance."

A waitress farewelled previous diners. She turned to us as they pushed past. "Table for two?"

She removed a band from her long, blonde ponytail, twisted her hair around her fingers, and replaced it.

"Yes please," said Fiona. "One by the window?"

The server showed us to two seats, dumped a menu in front of us, and rushed to deal with other diners.

I leant over the table, tilted my head, and paused.

"She's a kiwi," I said. "I've never been to a Chinese restaurant where the staff aren't Chinese."

"This is the West Coast. Of course she's a kiwi. Stop complaining and appreciate the view."

The hotel's architecture centred on an immense window in one wall, which gave a calendar-perfect perspective of the glacier.

"Look. The sunset on the glacier. The ice, it's orange."

"Stunning, isn't it? Where's the camera?"

"Um, in the car. I didn't think there'd be anything to photograph after dark. You'd never be able to recreate the scene. No-one would believe it."

I inspected the menu.

"What do you feel like?" asked Fiona.

"I'll have the beef in black bean sauce. What about you?"

"Sweet and sour chicken, I think. And some rice between us. And a vegetable dish. Stir-fried mixed vegetables in oyster sauce. How does that sound?"

"Great," I said. "And some of those prawn crackers to start."

The waitress passed with three wobbling dishes. I realized she constituted the entire staff.

"Excuse me? Can we order?"

"Sure. No problem. I'll be back in a tic."

She disappeared.

We waited.

"Stop tapping your fingers," said Fiona.

"I'm sorry. I'm starving, and the service isn't the best."

"Give her a break. She's about seventeen years old."

The server carried three more dishes. She returned, and I waved at her.

"Simon," said Fiona. "Stop making a scene."

The waitress pulled a pad out of her pocket.

"Yes?" she said. She glanced towards the kitchen. The sound of banging pots and sizzling came from behind the swing door.

"One beef in black bean sauce, one sweet and sour chicken, stir-fried mixed vegetables, and some rice please."

She wrote this down.

She glanced at the kitchen again. I heard a shout and more metallic banging. It sounded like the chef was wading knee-deep in woks.

"Is that all?"

"And some prawn crackers. Thanks."

She scribbled again, stuffed her pen and pad in a pocket, and strode away.

"I don't hold out much hope of this arriving any time soon," I said.

The kitchen door swung open, and the waitress dumped a basket of prawn crackers on our table.

"I take my comments back," I said. I picked up a prawn cracker and ate it. "These are good. Have one."

"I don't like them," said Fiona. "I'll wait for the main course."

The server approached with more dishes, and a bowl of stir-fried mixed vegetables materialized.

I wafted steam towards my nose.

"Let's wait for everything else," said Fiona.

The sun set, and I peered at the eerie view of the glacier in the dusk.

"The food's getting cold," I said. "Let's start."

We picked up spoons and dug at the vegetables.

"No chopsticks," I said. "Spoons and forks."

I hadn't seen the waitress for a few minutes, and the culinary steel band had completed recording their Greatest Hits album.

Some other diners finished their meals. They put their coats on.

I watched the server take their payment and disappear through the kitchen door.

We finished the vegetables.

The swing-door banged, and the waitress placed a bowl of sweet-and-sour chicken in front of us. She carried some other dishes to a nearby table.

I stared in the direction of the kitchen. "We could do with the rice. And the beef."

Fiona stabbed some chicken. She wiped sweet and sour sauce off her face with a paper napkin.

The waitress cleared plates at another table.

I cleared my throat unnecessarily.

"Could we have the beef, please, and the rice?"

She strode towards the kitchen with dirty plates.

We finished the chicken.

She returned and dumped our dish of beef on the table.

Fiona scooped up a forkful of the meat mixed with green peppers.

"We've been here over an hour, the dishes arrive one at a time, and I'm not sure we're ever going to see the rice," I said. "I'll ask her for the bill."

The waitress carried a pile of clean plates and set them out on a long table. I caught her eye.

"Could we have the bill, please?"

She tilted her head and looked at me. "Don't you want your rice?"

We felt our way back to the tent, cleaned our teeth in a cup of water, and wiggled into our sleeping bags. I tried to stuff my face in as well, but didn't want to suffocate.

Fiona snuggled against me.

"Last night of our trip," I said.

"It's gone so fast. I can't believe I start work the day after tomorrow. I'm looking forward to it. I haven't had a proper job in a year."

"I can't wait to do some more farming," I said. "It'll be winter soon and after that calving time. There'll be a heap more to learn."

"You need to earn some money, too. You could find work in the evenings?"

She yawned.

I wrapped my arms around her and closed my eyes.

≈≈≈

I was in the middle of an elaborate dream, where a kiwi had climbed into our car, and I was trying to feed it prawn crackers, while Fiona sped along the coast road decapitating possums as if she were in a sadistic rural New Zealand computer game.

DUGGA-DUGGA-DUGGA-DUGGA-DUGGA

I sat bolt upright.

What on earth was that?

DUGGA-DUGGA-DUGGA-DUGGA-DUGGA

I placed my palms flat on the ground and twisted my head left and right.

We needed to escape. Something was about to flatten our tent.

29. THE BIG PUNTER

The noise grew louder and receded into the sky.

Fiona turned over and rubbed her eyes. "I dreamt I was asleep on the runway at Heathrow."

"That was a helicopter," I said. "It sounded like it took off right outside the tent."

We heard another helicopter noise approach.

"I'm going to look outside," I shouted above the sound of the rotors.

I unzipped the tent and couldn't see any helicopters. The dugga-dugga sound continued from behind a row of trees.

"What are all these choppers for?" I asked.

"They fly up to the glacier. I think they land on the ice."

"Wow. Can you imagine? I'd love to walk on a glacier."

The rotor noise increased, and another helicopter took off.

"Have you ever been in a helicopter?" asked Fiona.

"I don't think I have."

"Me neither. Shall we see how much the flight costs?"

I pulled a bandanna over my head and zipped my woolly fleece to my neck. Our footprints indented the campsite grass, as we walked across the frost-dusted field.

We grabbed a hot drink and a toasted sandwich. Steam rose from the coffee, and the sandwich warmed me on the inside.

A sign displayed a picture of a group of people wearing red jackets, next to a helicopter. They stood against a backdrop of white mountain tops, under an immaculate, blue sky.

"Here we are," said Fiona. "The helicopter rides cost ninety dollars for a fifteen-minute look at the glacier from above, or two hundred dollars if you want to land on it."

"I'd love to land on the glacier. It must be such an amazing feeling, walking on ice, like a real mountain climber."

Fiona pulled some notes and coins out of her pocket.

"Hold out your hands," she said.

She counted.

"We have 207 dollars. And 35 cents."

"Is that it?"

"Yep. That's all the money we have left in the world. Until I receive my first pay. Which should be at the end of next week."

"What else do we need to buy before we return to the farm?"

"Nothing. We can skip lunch; these toasted sandwiches will keep us going."

"So could we fly in the helicopter?"

"We can afford for both of us to take the fifteen-minute trip that flies over the glacier. Or just one of us to land."

"I want to land on the glacier," I said. "But it won't be any fun without you."

Fiona took my hand.

"I'm happy for you to go by yourself," she said. "I'll snap some photos of you taking off."

My insides tingled.

You're the most special girl. I want to be with you for ever. Even if we haven't any money. Or any home of our own.

Fiona blinked at me, with her mouth in a straight line.

"You want to come too, don't you?"

One corner of her mouth turned up, and she raised one eyebrow.

"I would love to fly in a helicopter."

"Let's do the fifteen-minute one. That way we can both fly. We can come down here again one day and land on the glacier when we've more money. I'd prefer the flying experience with you, than the glacier landing all by myself. None of this means anything without you."

Fiona grinned, took my hands and squeezed them.

I picked her up and spun her around.

I've made the right decision. Plus, I'll feel bad all day if she doesn't come.

We entered the shop and approached a man sitting behind a desk. Tips of white hair peeked from under his beanie hat. He wore a red jacket with a mountain-top logo and the words 'Glacier Helicopters' printed under it.

"G'day, guys," he said. "Did you want to book a heli flight?"

The jacket rustled against his round face, and his white moustache moved with his words.

"Yes, please," I said.

The man pulled out a pad of forms and wrote the date on the top one.

"Name and address?" he asked.

"Fiona Wall and Simon Michael Prior. Hokitika."

"Wall?" he asked. "Are you related to Frank Wall?"

"I'm his daughter."

"Good bloke, Frank. I've a lot of time for your dad. Big punter. Makes my efforts look like chicken-feed. Tell him Jim from Franz Josef sends his regards."

"Thanks, Jim. I will."

"Did you want the fifteen-minute flight, or the thirty-minute with the glacier landing?"

"The fifteen-minute one, please," I said. "I'd love to land on the glacier, but we've only enough money for one of us to do that, and we both want to fly."

Jim sat up straight and peered left and right over my shoulder at the empty office.

He lowered his voice.

"Are you able to go right now?"

I heard rotor noise increase outside.

"Sure."

"The glacier landing chopper's about to leave. There are two seats left. If you run over to the helicopter, I'll let you have it for the price of the fifteen-minute trip. Special rate for Frank's daughter." He winked at Fiona.

"Wow," I said.

Fiona grinned.

She handed him 180 dollars, before he could change his mind.

Jim spoke into a walkie-talkie. "Stand by; two more for the glacier landing."

"Thanks, Jim," I said.

"No problem. Say hello to Frank for me."

We ran in the rotor noise's direction. A lady wearing an identical red jacket to Jim's held the side door of a white helicopter. She wore headphones with a mouthpiece, and I could see her lips move as she spoke into it. We occupied the last two seats, and the lady made a movement lifting both her hands to her ears, to indicate we should don headsets. She slid the door shut behind us, and I watched her step away.

The lady's red jacket became smaller, and she waved with her entire arm, as we took off.

"Good morning, everyone," said a voice in my headphones. "My name's Dale and I'll be your pilot today. Welcome to Glacier Helicopters. We'll be flying over the Franz Josef Glacier. We'll study the valley, and land on the glacier for a few minutes. You'll be able to walk on the ice."

Fiona squeezed my hand and smiled at me.

I wanted to say, "I love you," but I didn't know if every other passenger could eavesdrop through the headset, so I mouthed it. Fiona couldn't work out what I was attempting to tell her.

I could see the glacier through the front windscreen, over Dale's shoulder. I expected it to be pristine white, but the face of the ice displayed a dirty, grey, broad line, which puzzled me.

Dale continued his commentary. "Franz Josef glacier was formed in the last ice age, approximately twenty thousand years ago. It gouged a deep U-shape in what is now known as the Waiho river valley. Let's take a closer look at it."

At this point I doubted Dale's adherence to any safety procedures.

He banked the helicopter to the right, and we fell like a badly made paper plane thrown from an upstairs window.

Fiona held her stomach and grimaced.

A view of solid rock filled the front window.
I stared and pushed myself into the back of my seat.
We headed directly for the valley wall.
There was no chance Dale could pull away in time.

30. IRON MAIDEN

Dale hovered the helicopter in front of the Franz Josef Valley's side wall. If the windscreen had opened, we could have reached out and plucked one of the tiny, delicate ferns growing on the invisible rock ledges.

The other passengers opened their mouths wide, and I realized I'd done the same.

Dale ascended sedately, like a glass lift in a shopping mall atrium. He steadied the helicopter a short distance from the cliff. My head swam with a twinge of motion sickness. Fiona puffed her cheeks out and held her stomach.

The geology lesson continued.

"The Southern Alps are formed of 600-million-year-old greywacke rock with some schist," said Dale. "The glacier carved through it, forming the U-shaped valley we're in."

We cleared the upper lip of the valley side, and I glimpsed white mountain tops. Dale swung the helicopter in a circle, and we approached the glacier.

"The terminus and sides of the glacier are dirty grey, which surprises people expecting to see pristine, white ice," said Dale. "The colour's caused by the glacier gouging the rock and pushing fragments in front of it. It's known as the moraine."

Dale pulled back on the yoke, and we skimmed above the ice.

We hovered over a string of people roped together. I stretched my neck to see them. The man at the front waved at us with a large tool which I realized was an ice pick.

This is exciting. Real mountaineers.

"New Zealand has over three thousand glaciers," Dale continued. "The high rainfall in this area falls as snow at the top of the glacier, an area called the neve. New snowfall compresses the old snow into blue ice. The ice moves down the valley with gravity and creates crevasses under the strain of the movement. If you look out of your left window, you'll see a large one."

225

Dale considerately tipped the helicopter on its side, so everyone could obtain a good view. Fiona leant into me, clenched her teeth, and grabbed my arm.

We stared down the crevasse. The blue ice became blacker in its depths. I couldn't see its bottom.

Dale levelled the helicopter, and we ascended. I gasped at the all-round view of pure white snow interspersed with grey rocks. I understood what climbers meant when they said they were at the roof of the world. The peaks stretched in all directions, under a blue sky streaked with white, translucent vapour.

Dale circled and landed on a flat section in the middle of a Roman amphitheatre of mountain tops.

He turned to us and took off his headset. We copied him.

"Ten minutes here guys; don't stray too far from the helicopter." He grinned and winked. "Last week I saw a yeti up here, and I'd hate for anyone to be eaten."

He hopped out and opened the side door.

The cold hit my cheeks, like someone had slapped me with a frozen salmon. My feet scrunched on the ice and I sank slightly into it. I helped Fiona down.

I took a deep breath of clear, fresh, mountain air.

"Are your teeth cold?" asked Fiona. "I've never felt cold on my teeth before."

I turned to Dale.

"What's the temperature up here?"

"About minus ten Celsius. Reasonably warm today. No wind."

I scraped up some ice into a ball and made to throw it at Fiona. She didn't look impressed, so I put it down.

She took a picture of me with the helicopter.

I walked over to her and draped my arm around her shoulders. We turned and gazed at the jagged mountain tops surrounding us.

A few more metres, and Edmund Hillary and Sherpa Fiona will have conquered Everest. We'll plant the British flag. Our photos will be in newspapers across the world. Our names will live on forever. There are no mountains left to climb. We've climbed them all. We've conquered the biggest.

"Are you day-dreaming again?" said Fiona.

"I was thinking about Edmund Hillary and Everest."

"He's a New Zealander, you know?"

"Don't tell me," I said, "he's a racing friend of your dad's?"

Fiona laughed.

Dale shouted behind us. "A couple more minutes, everyone."

I took off my sunglasses and stared at the view. Fiona snapped some more photos.

The film ran out.

My eyes hurt from the glare, and I replaced my sunglasses on my nose.

"I still haven't seen any of this West Coast rain, Fiona. It's always sunny."

≈≈≈

Fiona dropped the tent into the car boot. "Two more hours' driving, and we'll be home."

"And you start work tomorrow."

Fiona sat in the driver's seat and turned the key. I jumped in beside her.

"Work, I know," she said. "It's been great having all this time off, but I'm ready for something new. Even if it isn't what I did in London."

"And we need the money," I said. "We've about 25 dollars to our names."

"Can you grab that now? We've almost run out of petrol."

Fiona steered into a garage forecourt, I put our last cash in the entire world into the tank, and we set off along the coast for home.

≈≈≈

Frank stood on the lawn in paint-splodge-decorated trousers.

"Welcome home," he said. "And welcome to your new residence."

He gave a satisfied smile and gestured at the old workers' hut. He'd repaired the hole in the side and painted the weatherboards cream, to match the farmhouse.

"Goodness," said Fiona. "That's wonderful, Dad."

I picked her up and carried her over the threshold. Frank had cleared junk away, and a bed, sofa, table, and two chairs remained.

"This'll be the same as when we lived in London," I said.

"It's about the size of our flat," said Fiona. "I need to christen the toilet. Hang on."

She entered the bathroom and exited two seconds later.

"There's no lavatory," she said. "Unless Dad's tacked on another room we haven't found."

I popped my head around the bathroom door. A shower and a sink squashed into a space the size of a Primark changing-room cubicle.

"Oh well," said Fiona. "We'll have to pee over at the farmhouse."

I gazed over her shoulder, out of the door, and earmarked a shrub for midnight emergencies.

She put her arms around me. "Our first home in New Zealand."

Phillip arrived on his motorbike and poked his head in.

"How's the hut?" he said. "It looks smarter than when I lived in it years ago."

"Phillip has some news," said Frank. He grinned. "Haven't you, Phillip?"

Phillip shuffled his feet and looked down.

"What's the news?" said Fiona. "Don't keep us in suspense."

"All right," said Phillip. "Adrienne's pregnant. You're going to be Auntie Fiona again."

"Fantastic," she said. "Congratulations."

"When's she due?" I asked.

"In November. The first scan's in a few days."

He took his hat off and scratched his head.

"I'd better repair the brakes on that tractor. See you later."

He stumped off towards the sheds.

≈≈≈

I returned from morning milking to find Fiona dressed in a dark-green suit, with a white blouse.

"Good luck at the new job," I said.

She looked in a mirror and applied lipstick.

"I must dash. Can't be late on my first day. Maybe you could look for work, Simon? There must be something."

She kissed me, jumped in our car, and sped down the drive.

I switched on the television. An annoyingly jubilant lady advised me that if I sent her four hundred dollars for an Eze-Train home gym, I would instantly have six-pack muscles to rival an Olympic weightlifter's.

What am I going to do for a job? Fiona's salary isn't enough to get ahead, even if we don't have to pay rent.

My guitar case glared at me, so I opened it, pulled out my instrument, and tightened the tuning heads.

Maybe some pubs or restaurants will pay me to play music in the evenings?

I strummed some chords and hummed along to a song by The Beatles.

I found a piece of paper and entitled it 'Guitar tunes.' Under the heading, I wrote 'Here Comes the Sun'.

I'm Noel Gallagher, striking the opening riff of 'Wonderwall' in front of thousands of adoring fans. They're all screaming my name. Some of them have queued overnight to buy tickets for my concert. Fiona's in the VIP area, watching from the side. My personal assistant brings her a champagne. Pride shines in her eyes, as she gazes at me across the stage. This is what I was meant to do.

Phillip drove past on his motorbike.

I put the guitar back in the case. This would take weeks of practice.

The rain began in the night.

Drops the size of watermelons smashed on the tin roof.

The noise woke us, and we both sat up in bed.

"I love this sound," said Fiona. "It reminds me of when I was a little girl. It feels cosy."

Cosy?

It sounded like we were trapped inside the snare drum during one of the faster-paced songs at an Iron Maiden concert.

Fiona turned away from me and snuggled under the duvet.

I groped for the bedside clock.

5:00 a.m.

I tugged on my farming clothes, shut the bedroom door, and turned the kitchen light on.

The pre-dawn revealed puddles and rivers submerging the farm tracks.

Coffee. Need coffee.

The rain drowned the noise of the kettle.

I held my hot drink and watched the sky lighten.

Phillip arrived on his motorbike, dressed in dark-green waterproofs. He wiped his eyes, opened the hut door, and said something which I couldn't hear.

The snare drummer performed a vigorous solo.

I cupped my hands around my mouth.

"Pardon?"

"I said, it's going to be a wet one today. Could you fetch the cows? They're in the second paddock along the track, before the creek."

I grabbed my wet-weather gear and pulled on my boots.

Jazz contemplated me, his head on one side.

"Come on, boy."

The rain ran down the hood of my jacket, along the sleeves, and dripped off my fingertips.

Jazz shook himself violently, sneezed, and jumped on the tray of the four-wheel bike.

The cows were pushed together like runners at the start of the Boston marathon. The matriarchs jostled for position, as I opened the gate.

I stared at my feet to shield my face from the rain, and I watched the hooves pass. When there were no more, I shut the gate, and followed the herd to the shed.

"..by Cutting Crew. You're listening to 93.1 Scenicland FM. We've severe weather warnings for all West Coast regions today and flood alerts for every river. Be careful out there, and stay tuned for more updates on the situation while you 'Take It Easy' with the Eagles."

Phillip attached the milking cups to the cows' udders.

I held my spray bottle and watched.

"Phillip, I'll take the cups off. I can do that part of the process now.

I chose a cow, removed the cups one by one, and hung them up. I removed a second set, then a third. Phillip rinsed them.

"How'd it go in John Parsons' rotary shed?" he asked.

"It was okay, but I prefer working here. The West Coast's more relaxed."

I sprayed the udders and opened the gate. The cows headed out into the deluge. I shut the gate, and new cows walked in. They glistened with the rain on their backs.

Phillip had his back turned.

I grabbed the milking machine and pushed a teat into the first cup of the front cow. It pulsed rhythmically and I slid the second one on. I missed the third, and the cup sucked at the cow's underside. I detached it and pushed the teat into the cup with my finger. The fourth followed.

I've done it. I've attached the cups to a cow. First step to milking all by myself.

Phillip pulled them off again.

I frowned and shrugged, with my palms facing upwards.

"What did I do wrong? I thought I'd attached the cups perfectly."

"You did," he said. "But she's on antibiotics, so her milk can't go in the vat. We have to divert it into a bucket."

"Oh no. Have I poisoned the entire morning's milk?"

"They won't notice that bit, I hope."

"How does the tanker driver know if the milk's acceptable?"

"It's tested at the factory. If they find antibiotics in it, they consider it contaminated and not fit for human consumption. They'll throw it out and then they don't pay us."

The final cows walked up to the milking machine.

Phillip attached their cups, took his baseball cap off, and scratched his head.

"What's wrong?" I asked.

"We're missing one," said Phillip. "Number 58. She's not here."

31. NUMBER 58

"We've milked 203 cows," said Phillip. "Where's number 58?"

"How do you know which one's missing? They all look the same."

"Did you check around the paddock?" he asked.

"I had a quick glimpse. I couldn't see far in the rain."

"I reckon you've left number 58 behind. Can you take the bike and have another 'quick glimpse'? The creek runs along the back of that paddock. Sometimes cows become stuck in the mud."

Jazz jumped on the four-wheel bike behind me.

I held the handlebars and drove along the track. The driving rain prevented me from looking forward, so I fixated on the ground in front of me. I progressed slowly.

The rain ran off my hands, up my sleeves and congregated in a low spot at my elbows. It stung my face as I opened the gate. I peered through the deluge and watched the trees bend in the wind.

No cows.

Jazz jumped off the bike and ran into the field.

He shook himself several times.

I inspected the edge of the paddock, along the fence line. Mud flicked up from the tyres.

No cows.

I checked the clump of trees in the centre of the paddock.

No cows.

I followed the creek at the back of the field and weaved among the dripping trees, following the bends.

Jazz found her first.

He barked ahead of me.

I rounded the corner and stopped.

A cow.

A water-logged cow.

I stepped off the bike and inspected her.

She turned around and gave me an expression of mild distaste, as if I'd heckled her speech at a Mother's Union meeting.

Her back legs squished into the mud, and her front legs bent in a kneeling position. She ate lush, creek-side grass and seemed relaxed.

I planted my feet wide apart with my hands on my hips.

Okay lady, you're coming with me, even if you don't want to.

How to move her? I could fetch Phillip.

Nope. This is my mistake and I'm going to put it right. What would Frank do if he were here?

Water sluiced between the creek banks. A dead branch swung around in the torrent and submerged.

If I don't free her and the water rises, she'll drown. I can't watch another cow die.

I revved the bike.

I shouted and waved my arms.

Jazz barked.

Number 58 returned to her breakfast.

I need a plan, and fast. Think, Simon, think. I need to be behind her, so I can frighten her up the bank. Standing in the creek's too dangerous; it'll sweep me away.

The cow squelched one leg and sank further into the mud.

What to do, what to do?

A dead tree lay nearby.

If I break off a branch, I can reach over and poke her in the backside. Not the nicest way to treat a lady, but preferable to drowning.

I hopped on the four-wheel bike, drove over the fallen tree, and snapped off a long, thin stick.

Jazz ran alongside me, as I dragged the branch back to the cow.

The water rose further up her legs.

I grabbed the thick end of the stick, leant out and tapped number 58's back end.

She gave me an annoyed expression and made the tiniest attempt to move.

Yes. This is going to work.

I tapped the cow's bottom again.

She shifted, but I couldn't reach far enough to give her a good prod.

I lay down on my front in the creek-side mud. The cold dirt seeped through my trousers.

The rain ran down the inside of my wet-weather gear. I shuffled forward on my elbows, like a camouflaged soldier easing under barbed wire. One of my boots came off and took my sock with it. Mud squished between my toes.

I reached out as far as I could over the creek, held the stick with two hands, swished it, and skimmed the cow's tail bone.

She gave me a bemused look.

I shook my fist and clenched my teeth.

"Damn you bloody cow."

I leant out further across the creek, swung the stick at the cow, missed, and toppled down the bank. I grabbed a gorse bush, and watched my other boot vanish in the water.

This activity alarmed the cow.

She wriggled, squirmed, and with a huge squelch reminding me of Fiona's grandmother serving trifle, number 58 freed herself. She scrambled up the bank. I heard Jazz bark.

I scrabbled out of the creek, slipping and sliding. Brown blancmange-like mud oozed between my toes, and blood ran from my gorse-scratched hands.

The cow trotted across the paddock and departed via the open gate.

I retrieved my sock and single boot and leant against the bike to put them on. I shook myself. If a competition existed for muddiest New Zealand farm employee, I was definitely a prize contender.

Jazz and I motored out of the paddock.

≈ ≈ ≈

Number 58 stood by herself in the shed, with the milking machine on her teats. Her experience didn't seem to have bothered her.

Phillip washed the yard with the big hose.

His jaw dropped as I squelched in.

He laughed.

"Stand there, Simon. Stand right there."

I clasped my arms in front of me and stood obediently in the centre of the yard, like a naughty boy who's walked into his mum's clean kitchen after a mid-winter game of football.

Phillip pointed the big hose at my chest. He rinsed off mud, creek weed, and cow poo.

"Turn around," he said. "Other side."

My boot filled with clean water. I braced myself against the flow.

"Go, and have a shower," said Phillip. "I'll finish here." He laughed again. "And find some new boots."

Frank read the racing pages.

Fiona and Angela watched a repeat of a British sitcom called *George and Mildred*. I remembered seeing the same episode as a boy.

I sat wrapped in a blanket and coughed. The rain sluiced down the living-room window.

Linda produced an elderly bottle of medicine, named Bonnington's Irish Moss.

"You won't be milking tonight, Simon."

"I can manage," I said, between sneezes.

"No you don't," said Linda. "It's all very well helping on the farm, but you're not to kill yourself. Go to bed. Phillip and Frank can do it."

I opened the kitchen door, shuffled down the path to our hut, and lay down on the bed.

I heard Phillip's motorbike drive past my bedroom window.

I dozed.

I heard Phillip's motorbike again, from the opposite direction.

I slept and heard nothing else.

≈≈≈

Morning.

Relentless, unending water washed down the windows.

I began to understand the West Coast's reputation.

A continual deluge that would have challenged Noah fell from the sky.

Fiona's side of the duvet was turned back. She brushed her hair in front of a mirror.

"Morning," I said, "did you sleep okay?"

"You slept well," said Fiona. "I moved to the sofa; you were making such a din."

"Sorry," I said. "I always snore when I have a blocked nose."

I pulled on my wet-weather gear and boots, opened the door, put my head down, and ran to the farmhouse.

Linda placed a cup of tea in front of me.

"How are you feeling?" she asked.

"Better, thanks. It must have been a 24-hour sniffle. I'll be all right for milking this afternoon."

"Oh, good," said Linda. "Frank needs to go to a meeting; he won't be home. Phillip can do it by himself, but it's quicker with two. I don't want to do it. My days of milking are behind me."

The kitchen door opened and slammed back on its hinges.

"Frank, shut the door! Everything's blowing around," said Linda. She picked yesterday's newspaper off the floor.

Frank kicked off his boots in the porch and hung up his wet-weather gear.

"How's it looking out there?" asked Linda.

"The creek's pretty high," said Frank. "I hope we can retrieve the cows."

"Why wouldn't we be able to?" I asked.

"When it floods, we can't drive any machinery over the creek to fetch them for milking. It's already too deep for your four-wheel bike; soon the tractor won't be able to cross, either."

"Have you thought of building a bridge?" I asked.

"I bought concrete piles for a bridge, decades ago," said Frank. "The truck delivering them became stuck driving over the one-lane section of Arthur's Pass, and it offloaded them by the roadside. They've been there ever since. I can't locate the receipt, and now nobody believes they're mine. The next time we cross the mountains, I'll show them to you."

I discerned the cow shed through the sheets of rain.

Puddles in the farmyard merged.

Fiona stood beside me.

"You're going to need a boat," she said.

"We used to have a canoe," said Linda, "but the possum eradicator man borrowed it and left it by the creek. The flood swept it down the river. We found it smashed up on the beach."

I considered the force of nature.

How we lived closer to its power on the farm.

How it influenced everyone's lives here.

How, when it rained hard, city folk could stay inside and watch television. Not try to canoe across flooded creeks to fetch cows.

"How long's the rain forecast to continue?" I asked.

"Should ease off by lunchtime," said Linda.

"It better do," said Frank.

≈≈≈

The rain pounded harder on the tin roof. Sheets of water drove diagonally across the paddocks. All farm work ceased.

We ate a sandwich on the sofa and watched the lunchtime news.

The weatherman announced dry sunshine for the whole of New Zealand.

Nearly the whole of New Zealand.

Westland barely received a mention.

"Gees, if anywhere else in the country had this amount of rain, the government would declare a major disaster," said Linda. "Us West Coasters have to grin and get on with it."

She picked up her book, slid her glasses on her nose and lay back.

I stared out of the window into the grey.

A flash of lightning startled me.

Out of childhood habit, I counted.

"One thousand, two thousand, three thousand."

A clap of thunder.

"The storm's three miles away," I said.

Lightning.

"One thousand, two thousand, three thousand, four thousand, five thousand, six thousand."

Thunder.

"Now it's six miles away. That can't be right."

"There are two storms," said Linda. She returned to her book.

The lights and television flickered and turned off.

"Power cut," I said.

RATTLE RATTLE RATTLE

"What the hell's that?" I asked. "It came from outside the house."

I peered down the hallway.

RATTLE RATTLE RATTLE.

The hair on the back of my neck stood up.

RATTLE RATTLE RATTLE RATTLE RATTLE

The noise came from the other door.

The front door.

The door no-one ever used.

32. HOPPY'S JET

"Everyone's here in the living room," I said. "Who's rattling the front door? Someone's trying to break in."

The clattering stopped.

Pause.

Scratch, scratch, scratch, scratch, scratch.

A different noise sounded from outside the kitchen.

Linda stood up, placed her glasses on the couch, and walked over to the door.

She opened it. Jazz entered and shook himself. He proudly wore a cat flap around his neck like a rapper's necklace. He sidled up to me, sneezed, sat, and looked up. The cat flap hung open under his chin.

I giggled, knelt down, and eased the flap over his ears and off his head.

"This always happens when there's thunder," said Linda. "Jazz becomes frightened, and he tries to break into the house through the cat flap. He can't fit, of course, so he ends up wearing it."

Linda grabbed a towel from the wash house and rubbed the dog. Jazz lay on his back and hid his eyes with his paws.

"He thinks if he covers his eyes, we can't see him," said Linda. "He knows he's not allowed inside, but I can't bring myself to throw him out in a thunderstorm. He's terrified of them."

≈≈≈

The power cut continued, and the afternoon gloom increased.

Linda found a torch.

"How d'you milk if the electricity's out?" I asked.

"We can't," said Linda.

Frank entered, dressed in a business suit and raincoat.

"I'm off to my meeting. See you later."

"You're driving in this weather?" I asked.

240

"If us West Coasters didn't drive in rain, we'd never go anywhere."

I watched him dash to his car. His tail lights dissolved in the mist.

The deluge eased to heavy drizzle.

The lights turned on again, and the television announced how desirable I'd be to swimsuit-wearing young ladies if I simply purchased a bottle of Old Spice aftershave. I blinked and pushed myself off the sofa. Jazz rolled over and stood up. He regarded me, with his head on one side, and his tongue out.

"Tea?" said Linda. "I'd better make it quickly, in case the power goes out again."

She flicked on the kettle and rattled cups.

I heard Phillip's motorbike pass.

The noise faded towards the creek.

Linda made the tea.

She produced a home-made slice.

The motorbike noise returned.

Phillip opened the kitchen door. He stood on the step in drenched wet-weather gear.

"Can anyone give me a hand?"

"What's happened?" asked Linda.

"I need to make sure the cows get back to the yard. They've found their way onto an island in the river."

≈≈≈

I scratched at my chin.

Oh no, did I do that? Are they supposed to get out to the river? Did I forget to shut a gate yesterday? When I retrieved the stuck cow? One rule. Leave a gate as you found it. Did I break the one rule? I can't remember.

"I'll come," I said.

I pulled on my raincoat, and boots.

Phillip started the engine of a tractor. The one Frank buried the cow with. The Massey Ferguson 174-4.

I hopped on the side.

Jazz ran along beside the tractor. He shook himself and sneezed.

241

We arrived at the creek.

Muddy water sluiced between its banks.

I watched a tree branch float past and wedge in the weeds. It spun around, freed itself, and continued down the creek.

"Can the tractor drive through?" I asked.

We have to reach the other side. I can't allow myself to drown the entire herd.

"One way to find out," said Phillip.

He glanced down at the dog. "Jazz, jump up here. You'll never swim across."

Jazz put his front paws on the tractor's step. I grabbed the scruff of his neck and pulled him up.

I put my arm around him. He wiped his wet head on me.

The tractor's front wheels submerged.

Phillip gripped the wheel and concentrated. "So long as it doesn't enter the air intake, we're okay."

The rear wheels entered the creek, and water rose up the tractor's red body.

The tractor eased over the stones. The flow pushed against one side. A stick lodged in the mudguard and disappeared under the tractor.

The front wheels began to exit.

Phillip increased speed and drove out. I let go of Jazz, and he jumped down.

Diluted sun showed through the grey. I removed my hood.

The river formed wide, dirty, brown channels. On the far side of the first one, the herd mooed urgently from a gravel island.

Phew. Some of them are still alive.

I tried to count them.

"Stay there, girls," shouted Phillip. He stepped off the tractor. "Stay there. Stay there."

The cows disobeyed him. A black-and-white stream of animals entered the muddy torrent and swam. Their heads stuck out of the water and made small waves. I watched, fascinated, as if I were viewing gnus in a David Attenborough documentary.

The matriarchs reached our side. Their legs and tummies emerged.

They splashed along the track and swam across the creek towards the farm.

I counted them.

I lost count.

"Jump on," said Phillip.

I hopped up, pulled Jazz with me, and we followed the herd.

I watched the line of cows entering the shed. Phillip walked in, and the milking machine hum began.

"..alerts are still in place for most rivers, but we're in for a spell of fine weather. You're listening to 93.1 Scenicland FM. Stay tuned, there's more great music coming up, right after these messages from our sponsors."

Phillip attached the milking machine to the cows. I counted them again. I lost count again. I watched the sight glasses, removed the cups, sprayed the ochre liquid and opened the gates.

The last cows walked out.

"Phillip," I asked. "How many cows were there?"

"Two hundred and four." He grinned. "Same as yesterday."

I shook my head, closed my eyes, and breathed out.

"Thank goodness," I said. "I was so worried the river had swept some away."

"Never happened yet," said Phillip. "They're more intelligent than you think."

≋≋≋

I poured a bowl of Nutrigrain and glanced out of the hut window.

A flock of aerial sheep drifted through a light blue sky.

Frank walked past, and I opened the hut door.

"What needs doing today, Frank?"

"You have a break. As it's a nice day, I'm going to pressure-wash the exterior of the house."

"D'you need any help?"

"It's a one-person job, really."

"I don't want to sit around doing nothing. There must be something you need help with."

"You could clear the driftwood from the paddocks again, now the water's receded. The flood dumped a load more. If you're bored. It's not an immediate urgency."

"No problem," I said. "Happy to help. Anything else?"

Frank raised his head and surveyed the area, to see if anyone could hear us.

He sidled up and bent his head to my ear. "There is something."

"Sure, what do you need?"

"A jockey friend of mine gave me a good tip. Could you pop into town and put one hundred dollars on Hoppy's Jet, running in race eight, at the New Zealand Metropolitan Trotting Club."

He darted his eyes around again, pulled two fifty-dollar notes out of his wallet, and handed them to me.

"No problem, Frank; I'll take the little car."

≈≈≈

I hadn't ventured into a betting shop before.

Three men sat at a high, central bench. They glanced at newspapers and watched televisions mounted under the ceiling, which showed different camera angles of assorted horses and a mass of numbers I didn't understand.

The door swung closed behind me.

I stepped over crumpled pieces of paper and cigarette butts and approached a lady behind a glass window at the rear of the premises.

I cleared my throat.

"One hundred dollars on Hoppy's Jet, please, running in race eight at the New Zealand Metropolitan Trotting Club."

I offered her Frank's money.

"Win, place or each-way?" she asked.

I pinched my bottom lip. "Erm, I don't know."

"D'you need a hand, boy?" I turned around. An older man wearing a trilby hat addressed me.

"Err, yes, please. I haven't done this before. I'm placing a bet for my girlfriend's father."

He dragged on his cigarette and flicked ash on the floor.

"Win's a win," he said. "If your horse comes first, you've won."

"Yep, that seems obvious."

"Place is a place. If you get first, second, or third, you've won. But you don't receive as much money, mind you."

"Okay, and each-way?"

"Best of both worlds. If your horse wins, or it places, you've won. The downside is the stake's twice as high."

I unfolded Frank's banknotes.

"I think I'd better pay for a win. Frank didn't say anything about places or each-ways."

"Frank, you say? Are you placing a bet for Frank Wall?"

"That's right," I said, "he's my girlfriend's dad."

The man stared at me and pulled a wad of cash from his pocket.

"What was the name of that horse?" he asked.

$$\approx \approx \approx$$

Fiona smiled at me from behind her desk. "Hello, I didn't expect to see you in town today."

"Your dad sent me to run an errand, so I thought I'd pop in."

"I'm about to have my lunch break. D'you want to eat something with me?"

We grabbed a hot sausage roll and a coffee from a bakery and sat on a beach-side bench. I watched the waves, as they crashed on the shore. Fiona threw a piece of pastry, and several seagulls congregated, flapped, and squawked as they fought for it.

"Guess what happened to me today?" she said. "Scenicland FM rang me and asked me to choose a song. I remember in London, I used to have to hang on the phone for hours to request a tune from Capital Radio. Here, the station calls you."

"What did you ask them to play?"

"'Broken Wings' by Mr. Mister. It's been going around in my head for a few days. Not sure why."

"I could think of worse places to live," I said. "You couldn't sit at the beach during your lunch break in London."

Fiona's eyes brightened, and she stared at the sea.

"It's wonderful to be home, and see Mum and Dad every day," said Fiona, "but I miss England. I miss our lives there. I can see I'll still be working in this same accounting job when I'm fifty. And we need more income. We can survive on my wages, but we'll never be able to save any money, or rent a home of our own."

"How can I bring in money?" I said. "There's no employment in Hokitika. And before you ask, I don't want to go back to Christchurch. I enjoy it here."

I watched the waves.

Driftwood washed back and forward with the motion.

"What about your guitar playing?" asked Fiona. "Have you thought any more about that? You could ask at some of the pubs and see if they'll give you a go. Dad knows several of the publicans. He'll put in a word for you."

"I can't play guitar for the rest of my life."

"You can do it for now."

She read her watch and stood up.

"I have to return to work. I'll see you at home."

≈≈≈

Frank leant a ladder against the side of the house and raised it several rungs, until it reached the apex of the eaves. He lay his pressure washer on the lawn, put one hand on his hip, shaded his eyes with the other, and gazed up at the roof.

I gave him the betting slip, and he stuffed it in his pocket.

"Time for lunch," he said, "then I'll wash the top of the house."

"I already ate in town with Fiona. I'll start on the driftwood."

We turned towards the driveway as a pickup truck pulled up.

Phillip leant out of the driver's window.

I walked over to the truck.

Adrienne sat beside him. Their two boys played with toy tractors in the back seats.

"Can you and Frank milk tonight?" said Phillip. "We're off to Greymouth Hospital for Adrienne's twelve-week scan. We should be back in time, but in case we're not."

"No problem," I said. "Take your time. Frank and I can manage."

Phillip gave me a thumbs up, spun the wheel, and accelerated. A cloud of dust signalled his departure.

I opened the hut door and changed into my farming clothes.

Jazz rode on the back of the bike with me. The little trailer trundled behind us. I glanced over my shoulder, to make sure it still followed as we motored through the creek.

The river had strewn a fresh selection of wood across the paddocks; branches, logs, and trees at odd angles. I picked up some smaller pieces and filled the trailer, lump by lump. My back twinged.

The trailer misbehaved again. I couldn't control in which direction it swung, so I gave up trying to reverse accurately and left it jackknifed at an angle close to the riverbank. I pulled the lumps of wood off one by one, stood up, and held my palm to the small of my back.

One more load.

I filled the trailer again and lay down in the paddock. Jazz crossed his paws, rested his head on them, and raised his eyebrows one at a time. The sun warmed my face, and I shaded my eyes.

Is this all I'm ever going to be? A driftwood farmer, incapable of milking the cows by myself.

A city boy, pretending to be a country boy.

A townie.

I wiggled into comfortable bumps in the field.

I closed my eyes.

I listened to the rapid rippling of the river at the edge of the paddock.

Rippling.

Ripples.

River.

Jazz nudged his nose against my head and woke me. He stretched his front paws, sat, and looked at me with his head on one side.

I pushed myself up.

How long have I been asleep?

"Come on, boy," I said. "Let's dump this load and go home."

Jazz jumped on the bike's tray.

I reversed the trailer as close to the edge as I could. It jackknifed.

I straightened up and reversed again. I peered over my shoulder.

"Jazz, move out of the way."

The trailer wiggled backward.

Left.

Right.

Left.

It pulled to one side.

I drove forward again.

If I can reverse the trailer right up to the edge, I can push the driftwood into the river. Easy.

I backed slowly. The trailer stayed straight.

This feels right. I think this is right. I must be nearly at the edge.

The bike jerked backward. I pulled the brake levers on hard and swivelled my head.

In slow motion, I watched the trailer full of timber detach itself from the bike and disappear down the riverbank, onto the gravel.

Shit.

I jumped off the bike and looked over the river's edge. The driftwood scattered across the pebbles, and the trailer lay upside down on top of it, like a child's discarded toy. Shallow water lapped at its side.

Now what do I do? I'll have to fetch the tractor to pull it out.

"Here, Jazz."

I drove the bike through the creek to the farmhouse.

My shoulders curved, and I looked down.

I've poisoned the milk with antibiotics, I've almost drowned the whole herd, and I've lost the trailer in the river. How am I ever going to be a farmer? I should go back to being a city boy and stop wrecking Frank and Phillip's business.

I stopped the engine and heard the cows, all mooing from behind a nearby gate.

Jazz sniffed at a dark-red stain painting the farmhouse footpath. A knife lay on the ground. Frank's ladder splayed at an odd angle across the lawn, next to his tin hat and pressure washer.

248

I frowned and tilted my head to one side.

What happened here?

I entered the kitchen door, which banged in the breeze.

A chopping board with a half-sliced onion lay on the kitchen bench, and a dining chair had fallen on its back.

Where is everyone?

I glanced at the kitchen clock.

4:15? Afternoon milking's at 3:30. What's going on?

The phone rang. I picked it up.

"Hello?"

"I've been trying to call you for ages," said Fiona. "Where have you been?"

"Out on the back paddocks getting rid of the driftwood. But I've lost your dad's trailer in the river, and there's no-one here, and the cows need milking, and everyone's gone, and…"

"Simon, stop. Listen to me. Dad's in hospital."

33. THE YOUNG FARMER

"Dad's been taken in an ambulance," said Fiona. "He was pressure washing the house, and he fell off the ladder and hit his head."

"Oh no, will he be okay?"

"I think so. Mum called from the ward. They've done a scan, and they're keeping him in for observation. He's got a nasty gash, and he'll have a sore head for a while."

"What am I going to do about the cows? They're all mooing from behind the gate. It's after four. Milking's well overdue."

"Where's Phillip?"

"He went to Greymouth with Adrienne and the boys. She's having her twelve-week scan. I told him Frank and I could milk tonight, and they'll have gone out for dinner or something. Fiona, what should I do? I've never milked the cows by myself. Hang on, there's a car coming down the drive. I'd better go. It might be Phillip."

I hung up and ran outside. The little car approached. Angela stepped out, with her school bag around her shoulders.

I put my palms on my hair.

"Angela, your dad's gone to hospital in an ambulance. He's hit his head. Phillip's not here, and I need your help. Can you milk cows?"

"Is Dad going to be okay?"

"It sounds like he will be; they're keeping him in for observation. So, could you help me milk? Have you done it before?"

"I've helped Dad and Phillip a few times, but not for ages. We'll manage between us."

I pressed my palms to my eyes.

"Thanks Angela, you'd better change your clothes. I'll fetch the cows."

I looked for the dog.

"Here, Jazz. Here, Jazz."

≈≈≈

The matriarchs pushed the gate open with such force it ripped out of my hands, and I fell.

I jumped on the bike and overtook them. This wasn't the way Phillip did it when he milked alone, but I was making this up as I went along.

I entered the shed. The first cows arrived and walked up to the machines.

I spun on my heels and waved my arms.

What's first? What's first? How do I turn on the milking machine? Phillip always does that.

A large button was mounted on the wall in a side room, near the milk vat. Another smaller switch next to it said 'radio'.

I shut my eyes tight, clenched my teeth, and pressed both of them.

The familiar hum filled the shed.

"..thank you, Patricia. The time is 4:34, we've nineteen degrees with a clear sky and an overnight low of eleven. Stay tuned to 93.1 Scenicland FM. Now, '(I Just) Died in Your Arms' by Cutting Crew."

Phew. Okay, okay. Cups on first cows. Careful not to drop the cups in the poo. Where's Angela? Oh no, I don't know if anyone's set the gates for the cows' evening paddock. Help! What do I do next?

I remembered how Phillip attached the cups. I put the first set on, one by one. I noticed milk pulsing through the sight glass.

I put on another set. And another.

I felt sweat soak my T-shirt.

This is taking too long. I'm going to be here all night. And which cows are on antibiotics?

Angela arrived.

"Angela, quick. Can you help me put the cups on? Do it like this." I demonstrated on the next cow.

"I know, city boy," she said. "I did this before you turned up."

"Okay, okay, we'll put the rest of the cups on, and I'll find a paddock for the cows this evening. Take the cups off in a few minutes. Don't worry if they haven't quite finished milking. And leave the gate until I come back. We don't want the cows loose."

I grabbed more cups and shoved them on udders. I wasn't sure if they were on correctly, but I couldn't pause to check.

Angela grinned at my panic.

I clenched my teeth.

"Here, Jazz."

The dog jumped on the back of the bike. We drove along the gravel track towards the creek.

Which paddock? Which paddock? Where do the cows go?

I searched for the lush green of a fresh meadow.

Dead Cow Paddock. I don't think the cows have eaten there since Christmas day.

I crossed the creek.

I opened the gate to Dead Cow Paddock, secured the electric fence across the track to ensure the herd wouldn't head for the river, and turned the four-wheel bike around.

Through the creek.

Careful. Slow, slow. Don't drown the bike.

Along the track.

I reduced speed and shaded my eyes with my palm.

Black-and-white animals approached me, their heads nodding up and down, and their breath steaming as they walked along the gravel.

I opened my mouth.

What's going on? Why has Angela released the cows?

I slowed the bike to a walking pace. The cows jostled past and headed to their fresh paddock.

In the distance, I saw Angela walk away from the shed, towards the farmhouse.

I frowned and twisted my head.

Where's she going? We've got milking to do.

I parked the bike and ran into the shed.

The cows stood, chewing the cud, with the milking machines attached to their udders.

Scenicland FM played 'Broken Wings' by Mr. Mister.

Phillip stood in the concrete channel between the two rows of cows. He detached a set of milking cups from an udder, hung them up, and rinsed them. He grinned at me.

"Hello, Simon. Everything going well here?"

≈≈≈

Frank sat on the sofa, a white bandage around his temple like a cartoon snake-charmer. A newspaper spread on his lap, with the television remote control on top of it. He tuned his radio, and the static cleared. I waited respectfully for the race to end.

"… and in front its Mistress Holmes, she's being overtaken by Annaleese Congo. Just Made It's losing ground to Eastwood Ladyship. They're on the final straight. Eastwood Ladyship's passing Just Made It. Mistress Holmes has nowhere to go. Annaleese Congo's in front, but Eastwood Ladyship's coming up on the outside. It's Eastwood Ladyship, Eastwood Ladyship, Eastwood Ladyship's achieved her fifth win. What a fantastic outcome for the jockey, Jim Curtin. Annaleese Congo gets second, and Mistress Holmes places third. We now go over to the next race at…."

Frank turned the radio off.

"Pppfff," said Frank. He screwed up a small piece of paper and threw it in the fireplace. "Not such a great outcome today."

"How are you feeling?" I asked.

"Average. I've lost my smell. Everything tastes of cardboard, or metal."

I looked at the carpet and clasped my hands together.

"Frank, I'm really sorry. I accidentally reversed the trailer full of driftwood over the riverbank. It's lying upside down on the gravel."

"Not a major eventuality. Phillip'll help you pull it out with the tractor."

Frank put down his newspaper and studied me.

"I hear you milked the cows by yourself."

"Angela helped me. And I only started them. Phillip came home, and we finished milking together."

"Yes, but you brought the cows in and commenced the process, without knowing any help was on its way."

253

"I had to do it. Fiona told me about your accident, Phillip was out, and I knew if I didn't milk them, no-one would."

"Well," said Frank, "we'd better open another bottle of Glenmorangie."

≈≈≈

Linda entered and dumped a laundry basket full of clean clothes on the sofa.

"Frank, what are you doing drinking whisky? The doctor said you can't have any alcohol. And can you taste it?"

"Hang on, Linda, have you heard what Simon did while I was in hospital? He milked the cows. All by himself."

"I just started them off. And Angela helped."

"I still think it's incredible," said Frank. He shook his head, his mouth in a straight line. "I'm glad you were present, to manage these occurrences."

Fiona walked in and put her arm around my shoulders.

"You should be proud of your young farmer," said Frank. "He's a credit to our family."

I lifted my head up at her and grinned.

Frank said I'm a young farmer. No-one's going to call me a townie again.

Frank raised his glass and chinked it against mine.

I took a sip of whisky.

I grimaced.

I might be a young farmer, but I still couldn't stand the taste of Glenmorangie.

EPILOGUE

On the 19th of August 1998, Robin Andrews, the Stewart Island Air pilot, took off from Halfmoon Bay, on the scheduled return flight to Invercargill airport.

The plane suffered double engine failure, and a mayday call was heard just before five o'clock that evening. Robin successfully ditched the plane in the sea, 2.5 nautical miles west of the town of Bluff, and he and the nine passengers escaped. The aircraft stayed afloat for some minutes after the landing. Due to some confusion as to the exact crash site, it took rescuers over an hour to reach the survivors. Five people were saved by the Coast Guard, suffering from extreme hypothermia.

Robin Andrews and the four other passengers perished, in the wintry, rough waters of the Foveaux Strait.

The cause of the crash was never resolved.

The author has donated to the New Zealand Coast Guard, in Robin's memory.

PLEASE REVIEW
THE SCENICLAND RADIO

If you enjoyed The Scenicland Radio, please consider leaving a review, to inform other readers of your experience. I've made it super-easy for you.

All you have to do is visit the link below or scan the QR code, and it'll take you straight to the right page.

Thanks so much, it means a lot to me.

Simon.

smarturl.it/sceniclandreview

SOUTH PACIFIC SHENANIGANS

What happens next to Simon and Fiona in their New Zealand adventures?

Will Simon finally learn to milk by himself, and does he achieve his dream of playing guitar in front of a crowd of adoring fans?

Will Fiona settle back in her native West Coast, or will the culture and history of Europe feel too great a pull to resist?

And will Frank ever persuade Simon to enjoy Glenmorangie?

Find out more about their New Zealand life, in the forthcoming third book from the *South Pacific Shenanigans* series, due for publication in 2022.

To be the first to find out about its release, and see what Simon and Fiona are up to now, why not sign up for Simon's monthly newsletter at:

simonmichaelprior.com

PHOTOS TO ACCOMPANY
THE SCENICLAND RADIO

If you'd like to see photos that accompany The Scenicland Radio, please head over to my website or scan the QR code and click the book's cover.

simonmichaelprior.com

DISCLAIMER

I have tried to recreate events, locales, and conversations from my memories of them. To maintain their anonymity, in some instances I have changed the names of individuals and places. I may have changed some identifying characteristics and details such as physical properties, occupations, and places of residence. Any mistakes are all my own work. SMP.

THE COCONUT WIRELESS

When Simon and Fiona embark on a quest to track down the Queen of Tonga, they have no idea they'll end up marooned on a desert island.

No idea they'll encounter an undiscovered tribe, rescue a drowning actress, learn jungle survival from a commando, and attend cultural ceremonies few Westerners have seen.

As they find out who hooks up, who breaks up, who cracks up, and who throws up, will they fulfil Simon's ambition to see the queen, or will they be distracted by insomniac chickens, grunting wild piglets, and the easy-going Tongan lifestyle?

Read the first few chapters FREE by visiting the link, or scanning the QR code:

Smarturl.it/look inside coconut

AN ENGLISHMAN IN NEW YORK

Have you ever wanted a first-hand glimpse into post-war 1940s New York?

When 21-year-old John Miskin Prior travelled by ship to New York in 1948, he had no idea he was going to meet and dine with the Roosevelts and the Rockefellers. No idea he would be among the first ever to see 'South Pacific' and 'Death of a Salesman'. No idea he would witness Truman's election victory, so unexpected, the newspapers were reprinted.

This eyewitness account of an English student living in New York for the incredible year of 1948 – 49 has been collated from his letters discovered after his death, and forms a unique account of the period.

Read the first few chapters FREE by visiting the link, or scanning the QR code:

Smarturl.it/lookinsideenglishman

An Englishman in New York

THE MEMOIRS OF
JOHN MISKIN PRIOR 1948-49
Transcribed and Edited by Simon Michael Prior

ABOUT THE AUTHOR

Simon Michael Prior insists on inflicting all aspects of life on himself so that his readers can enjoy learning about his latest trip / experience / disaster / emotional breakdown (insert phrase of your choice).

During his extended adolescence, now over forty years long, he has lived on two boats and sunk one of them; sold houses, street signs, Indian food and paper bags for a living; visited almost fifty countries and lived in three; qualified as a scuba divemaster; nearly killed himself learning to wakeboard; trained as a search and rescue skipper with the Coast Guard, and built his own house without the benefit of an instruction manual.

Simon is as amazed as anyone that the house is still standing, and he now lives in it by the sea with his wife and twin daughters, where he spends his time regurgitating his experiences on paper before he has so many more that he forgets them.

Website: **simonmichaelprior.com**

Email: **simon@simonmichaelprior.com**

Facebook: **@simonmichaelprior**

Instagram: **@simonmichaelprior**

Twitter: **@simonmichaelpri**

If you would like to receive a regular newsletter about Simon and his writing, and be the first to find out about new releases, please sign up to his mailing list here:

simonmichaelprior.com

ACKNOWLEDGEMENTS

A big thank you to Victoria Twead and all the members of the Facebook group 'We Love Memoirs', for befriending me, encouraging me, educating me, reassuring me, and driving me forward.

This book would not have been possible without the help of the following people: Linda Wall, for helping me fill in details when my memory failed me. Paul Shannon, for expert advice on small plane aviation, for ensuring I correctly recorded a Piper Tomahawk's start-up procedure, and correctly described aircraft radio calls. My amazing beta readers: Alyson Sheldrake, Judith Benson, Julie Haigh, Kandy Ostrosky, Kevin J D Kelly, Lisa Rose Wright, Pauline Armstrong, and Susan Jackson, you guys rock, and your feedback improved the final result so much. Thank you to Victoria Twead, Meg LaTorre, David Gaughran, and Dave Chesson for informative courses, tips and useful tools. Thank you to Jeff Bezos, for giving independent authors a platform on which to publish our writing. And thank you so much to Fiona, I couldn't have done it without you.

WE LOVE MEMOIRS

Join me and other memoir authors and readers in the 'We Love Memoirs' Facebook group, the friendliest group on Facebook.

- Chat with memoir readers and authors.

- Make friends all over the world.

- Get book recommendations.

- Win Books.

- Have a good laugh.

www.facebook.com/groups/welovememoirs

Made in the USA
Monee, IL
24 February 2022